Living
Creatively

BOOKS BY ADRIAN VAN KAAM

Adrian van Kaam

Living Creatively

Formerly published as Envy and Originality

Dimension Books · Denville, New Jersey

ISBN: 0-385-06990-1
Library of Congress Catalog Card Number 70–116260
Copyright © 1972 by Adrian van Kaam

In memory of my friends

Rinus and Jerry

Who were original men

ACKNOWLEDGMENTS

I want to express my gratitude to my colleagues Dr. E. J. van Croonenburg and Dr. S. A. Muto for their many suggestions without which the content and expression of this book would have been less balanced, fluent, and precise.

CONTENTS

Chapter Five: Original Living in an Unoriginal World   139

Chapter One

Envy and Originality

At the end of the last world war, I was hiding in a small Dutch village. The leader of the Resistance, a mailman, was a person of daring and cunning. He knew how to outwit the enemy. The few who were aware of his activities spoke about him with awe. Pete had always been a man of original force and integrity, but it was only the war that revealed him in a way no one had foreseen. We loved to discuss Pete. Was he an original man before the war? Would his originality have come to the fore without the war?

Originality is like a unique mark each man receives at birth. It is his latent ability to be himself in his own way. A person may or may not be faithful to that power in him. Pete always seemed to have been himself, as a boy in school, as a mailman, a young husband and father. Now he was himself as a leader of the Resistance. It was still the same Pete, but he showed himself in a new light.

Whether or not a man allows his uniqueness to become a source of growth is up to him. If he does, we can ask ourselves, what form will his originality take?

What his originality will be concretely at a certain moment of his life has a lot to do with the situations in which he finds himself. Special occasions invite him to be his unique self in a special way.

Pete's whole life could have been spent taking care of his family and carrying the mail. He would have done this in his own way and been good at it. As a man faithful to his originality, he would have become more and more rich and unique as a person. But war came. It put Pete in an unexpected position. He responded to this new challenge as he had done to the demands of daily life before the war. He was simply himself, only now as a leader in the Resistance. This situation, however, brought other dimensions of his originality to the fore. It compelled him to develop new skills and attitudes. These did not grow in isolation from his initial originality; rather, they expanded his original power, his unique "I am able to." During the war and in some ways after it, Pete was able to be his original self in a different and more expanded fashion than before this experience.

Initial Originality, Historical Originality

A man's history thus has something to do with what his originality will be like. We could call his originality, as it manifests itself at certain moments of his life, a historical originality, an originality which developed during his life history up to this moment. Historical originality differs from initial originality. The latter is merely the possibility of being myself in a certain style which I receive as my birthright.

In the beginning this gift is a mere possibility. A person's history will tell what he does with it; whether he buries this gift or lets it come to life; how he develops his originality in response to challenges met by him.

I have a friend whom I consider a great man. To me he is impressive because he is true to himself. He may not be as outstanding in the eyes of his family. They may have wanted him to be less himself and more like themselves— enterprising businessmen, social minded and philanthropic.

In a few generations they worked themselves up from regular workmen to captains of industry—people to be admired in their own right, men who allowed their own gifts to expand in response to the situations they faced in their lives.

My friend was not like his family. Of course, this fact would not make him great. The question was, how faithful would he be to his own gift? The answer to this question would make or break him as a man.

We do not know immediately at what we can be best. We become vaguely aware of certain likes and dislikes. These are not passing fancies. They come back again and again, even if we try to smother them. To what kind of life these inclinations point we may not yet know. Only in the course of life may we discover which styles of action make it easier for us to be faithful to our original gifts. We may also find out which life forms make it more or less difficult for us to remain true to ourselves.

For my friend it became clear that it would be difficult to be true to himself as a captain of industry, a banker, or the president of a company. He found himself interested in ranching and in writing novels.

One could ask what has happened to my friend's initial originality? It first revealed itself to him in likes and dislikes, indefinite and confusing. It made him feel different from others. He tried to ignore these spontaneous inclinations. Some of them disappeared. They proved to have been momentary impulses, fleeting impressions. Other propensities returned tenaciously. They proved to be truly and lastingly his. He began to discover also that he could be faithful to himself in various roles. If necessary he could live each position in his own fashion. Indeed, no role imposed on us compels us to betray who we are. Nevertheless certain positions in life give more scope than others for the unfolding of our personal gifts. The broader expression of our originality will in turn more easily affirm and deepen what we are.

My friend thought it over; he tried out many things. As a result, his vague inclinations became more definite. He began to feel how his personal bent could express itself more easily in certain ways of life. His originality now began to mean concretely that he felt more like being a rancher than a captain of industry, more like being a novelist than a banker.

To give a definite direction to my spontaneous inclinations is a first step. It is the beginning of actual original living in my everyday situation. But this first orientation is not enough. It is one thing to have the right insight and inclination. It is something else to realize such feeling and insight in thought and action.

To make originality a guiding principle in daily life, it is not enough to know what road I should take among the many possible roads offered to me. I must walk that road and keep walking. What up to now is only insight, and inclination must become a persistent and effective willing.

It was not enough for my friend to will at one or another occasion to be a rancher and a novelist. He had to will this intention enduringly. He had to work at it consistently. Only then could his potential be realized in some particular way. Realizing it in his actual life, he realized in his person the originality that was previously only a possibility. Insight and drive to be oneself in a concrete way in this world must thus be raised to a higher plane: that of constant effective willing.

Originality and Self-Motivation

My initial originality must be transformed into a concrete force that will shape my life realistically. I need an operational originality that becomes a driving power within me. What is that concrete guiding force? It is a fusion of many elements—an integration of guiding insight rooted in my experience of self and situation, of stimulating drive, of persistent effective embodiment of my will in concrete daily action. Have we a name for such an operational source of original action in man? We could call it "motivation." Not motive. A motive can be incidental, such as the motive to buy a lawn mower or a new car. Self-motivation means always a more lasting orientation of man. Motive may also refer at times to something external. Many motives are offered to us by people who try to convince us that we should buy something. Such motives are not yet mine as self-motivation is. I may weigh them as possible motives without ever making them mine.

Motivation is thus a fundamental enduring motive that has become an inner force that shapes my life continuously. Motivation can also internalize and transform new motives offered to me. In the process of appropriation, one or the other motive becomes transformed by my uniqueness.

Say somebody offered my friend a motive for ranching. He told him that ranching was more conducive to ease of mind than banking. My friend pondered this piece of wisdom. It made sense to him. As such, however, it was not enough to compel him to change his life. You don't put your future at stake simply because a certain kind of life promises you more ease than another.

My friend considered this motive in light of his originality. He thought about the uneasiness a man of his bent would have to bear with if he were to assent to the vocations proposed by his family. He may have balanced the hardships of ranching against the advantages it held for the unique kind of person he was. The motive "ease" obtained a personal meaning for him during these considerations. The somewhat simplistic and general motive offered to him was deepened and transformed, permeated by personal meaning, when brought in contact with the concrete demands of his personal gift.

We may call this inner direction not simply "motivation" but "self-motivation." Why? My friend could have falsi-

fied his life under family pressure. His family was motivated
to serve society by leadership in the business world. They
had an impressive record. He himself saw what great things
this motivation had done for them and society. How tempted
he must have been to follow in their footsteps. He could
have adopted their motivation. The only trouble was it
would not have been his. It would have been an "alien" motivation. He would have lived by the motivation of others—
a stranger to himself. Countless people fall into this trap.
The family motivation would have secured him a respected
but borrowed life. It would have destroyed him as a person.

Self-Motivation and Cultural Motivation

The initial originality, given to everyone, remains in many a
mere possibility. They never reach the stage of transform-
ing their latent uniqueness into an operational uniqueness
that enables them to live their own lives. Or, to say the same
thing, many never come to self-motivation. Self-motivation
is in tune with my originality. A specific self-motivation
may have come to me initially from the outside. I find embodied in my culture a variety of motivations. Such motivations are its shaping force. But I should not blindly take
over any motivation that I see alive in my culture. Cultural
motivations should become mine, but they can only become
mine in two ways.

First, I must select those cultural motivations that tie in
with my personal bent. I may highly appreciate other motivations. I may foster them in others. This does not mean that
I must make these motivations a shaping force in my own
life. I may support gifted composers who are deeply motivated to express their originality in musical creations without myself being motivated to be a composer.

Secondly, I must make a chosen cultural motivation thor-
oughly my own. I must root it in my uniqueness. I must allow it to be pervaded by my initial originality. Usually this

is a spontaneous action, not to be disturbed by undue attention. I must not meddle with this process by anxiously imitating others who live similar cultural motivations successfully. The cultural motivation I appropriate is in some way the same in them and in my culture, but it is also different. It undergoes a subtle transformation when it becomes the instrument of my own originality.

My friend wanted to be a novelist. As a matter of fact, he is now both a rancher and a novelist. His motivation to be a novelist would be unthinkable without an already existing cultural motivation. One has to live in our kind of culture to be motivated to write novels. An Eskimo, a head-hunter, a Pygmy—as long as they are encapsulated in their respective cultures—cannot be motivated to become novelists. My friend had to find in his culture the motivation to be a novelist. The crucial thing was that he made this cultural motivation his own. The writing of novels and the life of the rancher were a task and a life style which would enable him to live out his given originality. He also made this cultural motivation his own in the sense that he permeated it with his uniqueness. He was motivated not simply to write novels, but to write novels that would express his unique views and feelings.

A good love story is as old as mankind, yet it never bores us for it is always as new as the man who wrote it. My friend motivated himself to live the life of the writer not in blind conformity to a set pattern but in the way best suited to his personality. As a consequence, his self-motivation resulted in his own style of writing and his own style of ranch life.

Inventiveness and Originality

When we hear the word "originality," we do not usually think about people who live their lives personally but inconspicuously. Original persons are for us inventive people who dream up new kinds of entertainment, design new models of cars, or devise styles of dress different from those of the past. Inventiveness, however, is not necessarily rooted in personal originality. This is so true that I usually cannot tell much about the personality of an inventor from the thing he invents. My light bulb does not give me much insight into the inner life of Thomas Edison.

An inventor may be so fascinated by his work that he forgets to dwell on the meanings of human life that emerge outside his field. I may be most inventive as a designer and most unoriginal as a person. I may be alive as a manager and dead as a man. On the other hand, I may live an original life in the personal sense without being inventive at all.

The kind of inventiveness that insures increased production and consumption may be well rewarded. Inwardness—which enhances the quality of life and makes original experience possible—may be looked upon as a waste of time. Inventiveness may be fostered, while inner living is frowned upon. The inventor may receive social benefits, status, and position whether or not he is original as a human being.

When I see how successful the inventor is, I may try to appear like him. I may show off ideas, attitudes, and mannerisms that are not really my own. I merely imitate what seems to look original. My words and acts do not flow from my true self. They express and promote what I am not. Make-believe originality deforms me as a person. I am no longer moved by an inner awareness of what I uniquely should be. All that may move me is my desire to create a public image of originality. I am no longer self-motivated. I am moved instead by public motives, by fame, money, popularity, success.

Such motives may play a role in my motivational life. They do not necessarily exclude self-motivation. But if self-motivation would be absent, my originality would be absent too. Selfhood or human originality is uniquely motivating. The "original man" is the "self-motivated man." The moment self-motivation is lost, originality is lost too. The moment

self-motivation is regained, originality is restored. Originality
and self-motivation are two sides of the same coin.

Today there is a cry for more originality. Many who seek
originality try merely to be inventive or conspicuously creative outwardly. Meanwhile they neglect to live out of their
real originality. To be original inwardly means a good deal
more than assuming a superficial stand of imitation or reaction. A person can be original without being outwardly different. A person can be outwardly different without being
inwardly original. The original man need not invent new
forms of life or display unusual talents. He may simply do
what many others do in his environment. His originality
shines through not in *what* he does but in the *way* he does
it, not in the customs he *has* but in the way he *lives* them.

Reaching Self-Motivation

Why is it that in so many people initial originality remains
asleep? Why don't they actualize originality through self-
motivation?

Not long ago I took a cab. The driver was a cheerful fellow. I was touched by his care for his job, his cab, his passengers. He obviously liked his work. He told me about the
improvements he was thinking about for his cab, for his
work schedule, for the handling of his passengers. And, not
unexpectedly, he gave me a piece of his philosophy of life.

"I've been driving a cab for twenty years now. I like it. I
could have had other jobs, better paying, more fancy. But
the thing I like best is driving a cab. It just seems to fit the
kind of guy I am. I'm happy in my job. You know why?
Because I'm doing what I feel I can do best. I stay happy
because I don't make comparisons. No sir, not me. I don't
compare myself with the guys who have other jobs, the fancy
ones I mean. People who are always comparing themselves
with other people can't stay happy for long."

The cab driver told me many more things about himself

and his business. What struck me most was his remark that people who are always comparing themselves with others cannot stay happy. Are people in our age inclined to compare themselves with one another more than people in other ages or other cultures? Why should comparing yourself with others make you less content? These were the questions that crossed my mind. I tried first to figure out what comparing yourself with others means today.

The Problem of Comparison

If I compare myself with somebody else, I ask myself how far I resemble him. A woman may be anxious to know whether she plans on wearing the same dress to the dance as her friend. A man uncertain of his masculinity may ask himself whether the other guy can play as many holes of golf, down as many drinks, drive as fast. In a company every employee may be comparing himself with his colleagues: "What is he making now? What is his chance of promotion? Will he get a bigger raise than I? Is he more in with the boss than I?"

All these examples point to the fact that I can compare myself with others only in aspects of life that are comparable to begin with: such things as dress, driving skills, salary, promotion, favor with the boss. None of these things tell me what a man really is.

I cannot tell the uniqueness of a man from the house he can afford, the money he makes, his adroitness at bridge or golf. These talents tell me something about his technical skill, cleverness, zeal, or cunning. They leave me in the dark about what makes him a person different from anyone who lived before him or will live after him.

To compare is to look for what is alike or what differs in degree while still remaining basically the same in kind. We both have money coming in; the amount may be different. Both women wear evening gowns; the design and colors may not be the same. Both men play golf; their skill may vary. But the essence of uniqueness is precisely that it cannot resemble anything else. Unique means that there is only one of a kind. Uniqueness is incomparable by its very nature.

To meet a man in his uniqueness is to meet him in that dimension where he cannot be compared with others. People who are always comparing themselves are really not interested in meeting other people and themselves personally. They substitute for encounter a far easier procedure. They abstract from the person some superficial side that can easily be compared. They let this part stand for the person as a whole. This is Mr. Johnson. Great guy. He makes a big pile of money. He drinks like a fish, sleeps like a bear, and has an $80,000 home. None of these attributes familiarizes me with the stirrings of Mr. Johnson's soul. I know only where Mr. Johnson stands in comparison with other fellows in regard to housing, money making, and the capacity for sleeping and drinking. What is worse I may be inclined to rate my own worth on the same scale. I may feel great when my friends declare in awe that I can outsleep, outdrink, and outdistance Mr. Johnson.

People who are always comparing themselves do not meet one another as persons but as collections of quantifiable characteristics. They do not value one another for their original selves but for attributes that do not necessarily tell us anything about their uniqueness as human beings. They do not even meet themselves as persons. They reduce themselves and others to a set of measurable statistics. They do not want to hear about the rest. They ignore it. They make fun of it. Everyone is leveled out. No one is allowed to be who he is. Each man is fitted into the measurable, comparable categories set up by that anonymous master of leveling—public opinion.

Are people today more inclined to reduce themselves to a set of comparable statistics than people in other times and other cultures? It may seem that way. Our culture is built upon a consistent use of one of man's rational functions, namely that of abstraction. A most useful function, to be sure. Abstraction, among other things, is the art of taking away from a person all that is unique to him. Then we retain only those things that make him comparable to all other men. This function of thought is necessary for the smooth organization of people.

More importantly, by measuring the comparable skills and output of people, we can play them against one another. We make people aware that promotion in any commercial enterprise depends on outdoing the other on the measurable scale of production, of pleasing the public or the boss, of saying the right things. Soon people are falling all over themselves to outdo each other. The organization will then get the best out of them. As a result, output will be higher. Society seems to benefit, at least in certain measurable dimensions.

Because of its success, the principle of comparison spreads to other organizations. Take a church. Who asks himself about the unique intimacy of Mr. Peterson with the Lord? Who is interested in the prayer life of Mr. Peterson? What interests us most is: "How often does he go to church? How active is he in our organizations? How much does he put in the collection basket?" Some congregations even devise a system of open donations to be published in the weekly bulletin. Everyone can compare himself with everyone else and see exactly where he stands on the scale of contributions.

Our culture seems to thrive on the spirit of comparison. Why knock it? It works. What more do you want?

My cab driver seemed to hint that people who live lives of comparison cannot stay happy. Is the opposite not true? Aren't people upset if they cannot label somebody as a leftist, a rightist, a middle of the roader, as a psychologist or philosopher, as religious or atheist, as good or bad, as for or against something? Without such labels most people seem at a loss. They feel helpless. They are asked to do the impossible: to accept a man on basis of his inner worth, not as the representative of some category.

Labels are like the blades of scythes ready to level any man who sticks out as unusual. But in the case of an original person the easy labels don't work. The incomparable man is a nuisance. He'd better hide his originality or else! How then can my cabbie say that people are unhappy when they keep comparing each other? He must be talking about a special kind of unhappiness.

What happens when I keep comparing people? Success in the eyes of society is the precarious yardstick against which I measure their worth. But the yardstick I apply to others is like a boomerang. I begin to suspect that I too am the object of similar estimates. I begin to confuse my real value with what society says is valuable. I become anxious about what I look like in public. I am no longer carefree. I lose my quiet sense of self-possession and self-appreciation.

Can you really feel happy if no one ever meets you as the person you are? If you are valued only for your skills? If you always meet some people who will outdo you no matter how many promotions you get? If you feel the stress of having to look better than others in your job, neighborhood, club, or church? If you have to hide your originality because people resent the fact that it falls outside the categories of social comparison? If you meet people who are only too ready to make you feel how poorly you fare on the social scale in comparison with them? Does it not pain you to be identified with the kind of social success that cannot represent your original self?

Think for a moment about what happens to a movie star who has been chosen not for her capacity as an actress but for some measurable quality, such as her sex appeal. She is applauded by the public not for what she is but for an attractiveness which by no means represents the whole of her person. She becomes a symbol. Public relations men begin to piece together an image for public consumption. This image may have little or nothing to do with the real person. She must meet people on a superficial or make-believe basis.

This star may succeed in repressing her real personality, in telling herself that she is happy because she is adored for what she is not. She may even begin to believe that she is what she is not. But some day she may begin to taste the unhappiness my driver was talking about. Under her public image, she may discover a glaring emptiness, a paralyzed original life. She may be unable to sleep because of this terrifying emptiness. She may be horrified by the utter loneliness of her real self—never met, never recognized, never loved as she is. Despair may overwhelm her. She may end by committing suicide. Of course, she is an extreme case; nonetheless she is a symbol of the fate of man in an age of comparison.

My wise cab driver knew this so well. He knew he would be asking for unhappiness the moment he compared himself anxiously with white-collar workers, businessmen, storekeepers, insurance agents, with all kinds of people who might have done better than he in terms of the criteria of success held up by society. My cab driver was doubtful, however, if they had really done better in light of the criterion of their own originality. He suspected that he too could have succeeded in any of these jobs. He was a clever man. He could have made it. But would he have been happy? Could he have been the kind of man he happened to be? Wisely he kept his eye on the inward dimension, the incomparable one. He was delighted that he had found his niche in life. The same attitude helped him to be a prince for all of his passengers. He was a person who kept his dignity, the dignity of a man who knows his original worth above and beyond any standards of comparison society may apply to him. He looks at others not with an envious eye that frantically measures and compares but with respect. He is not disgruntled because they seem to do better than he.

Self-Motivation and Public Opinion

The man who respects his own originality has a respectful
eye for the originality of others. He meets each person as
unique. He rejoices in somebody's social accomplishments,
academic degrees, cultivated manners, all the time aware that
none of these reveals the unique humanity of a person. He
meets the other, above and beyond these accomplishments,
as a fellow human being. The other may be threatened or
delighted by this approach, depending on where he stands
in relation to his own originality at this moment of his life.

What is the basis of the standard by which we compare
each other? Often it is the opinion of the public.

No one can tell you concretely who the public is. It is
everyone and no one, that is, no one in particular. It is everywhere and nowhere, that is, nowhere in particular. At times
I am part of it. At other times I am no longer immersed in
the public; I am myself. Who precisely is the public? It
stands for all who look at TV, listen to the radio, read the
papers, eye the billboards along the highway, glance at
advertisements in the bus or at window displays in depart-
ment stores. The public is a generalization. It is a word for
an ever-changing number of people in their anonymity.

What moves the public *as public* is not self-motivation.
Self-motivation is the extension of my originality. It is that
which makes me more than the public. What moves the public is not even motivation as such. A particular group, such
as family, club, school, can be motivated together to do
something. The public is not a specific group. As merely a
part of the public, I am not associated with any definite
group of people whom I know, who subscribe to certain
enduring principles and projects. The public is that always
changing, amorphous, anonymous mass that feels important
and powerful because of mere number. Public opinion is felt
to be exceedingly valuable. Nobody knows precisely who

holds this opinion, yet it has a hold on man's imagination because the public somehow seems to cherish it.

If the public is not motivated in the true sense of the word, what then must we call those fluctuating movements of public sentiment? Perhaps "reflexes" is a good word. There is no lasting orientation in public sentiment. What the public adores today, it may despise tomorrow. Public sentiments are like fashions. Each one is enthusiastically given up for the one that presents itself as the latest. Words like "new," "modern," "in," "progressive" work like magic on the public. As soon as someone is able to convince the public that something is the latest, a reflex sets in. The big amorphous body of the public begins to quiver with excitement. Everyone seems to hunger for the latest.

Another key word in the public sphere is "success," meant here as measurable accomplishment. If you can convince the public that some person, enterprise, or thing is measurably successful, you have made it. A best seller becomes more of a best seller simply because it is known as a best seller. Some salesman may announce on TV and in the newspapers that a publication is a best seller. If he states his case convincingly, it may become a best seller. The content is not too important. Neither is the style. It has to be readable, easy to grasp, capable of satisfying the curiosity of the consumer. But for the rest, it may be shallow. The thing that counts is that it be known as a best seller. One day this best seller may be religious testimony, the next day a sex manual. The buyer may read neither one nor the other. The buying of the religious work does not prove in the least that the buyer is religious, nor does the buying of the sex manual demonstrate that the purchaser is a scurrilous fellow. Both purchases demonstrate one thing: the one who buys a publication *merely* because it is a best seller may well be a member of the anonymous public, a man moved by the reflexes that periodically pulsate through the public body.

There is no room for self-motivation within the public

sphere. A self-motivated man who would question the latest publication, song, dress, or movie on basis of his original feelings might be dubbed a party pooper by the public. Sad for him if these people discover that he is content with being himself. He may remind them vaguely of their own, now lost originality and they have no desire to be reminded of that.

The anonymous person relishes the reflex life of the public. He wants to be overwhelmed by media that feed his need for the newest, the most successful, for whatever flatters his feelings of cleverness and importance. With little or no trouble, he can be in with the latest; all it takes on his part is a simple reflex of identification and imitation.

For the original person the message is clear: Don't remind the anonymous person of self-motivation. You may make him angry and afraid. Afraid because self-motivation invites him to stand alone, all by himself, separated from the rest of the crowd. Your self-motivation reminds him of his inner emptiness and makes him envious of your inner richness. His response may be one of leveling envy. He may want to level you down until you become a mere number that, added up with all the other numbers, equals the same anonymous public.

Envy of originality leads to envy of comparison. The inner content of one's uniqueness can never be envied, for uniqueness is precisely that which nobody else can be. It is not the same with measurable quantities. It belongs to the essence of these quantities that many people can have them in various degrees. They can be compared. Therefore, a society that lives in comparison is a society that is bound to live in envy. Ours is an age in which we are prone to envy those who do better on the scale of comparable skills and fortunes than we ourselves; it is an age even more envious of the few who manifest faithfulness to their own originality in an unoriginal world.

Envy of Originality

When envious, I feel bad about something good in another because it is not mine. A value lacking in many of us is the courage to live our own lives. Those who are faithful to themselves may evoke envy in others. What is envy of originality?

Two roommates, Jane and Peggy, go to a dinner party. Both are well mannered, nice-looking, pleasant to talk with. While Jane says all the right things, she somehow lacks spontaneity. Peggy makes similar remarks, yet, shining through them, is the sparkle of her personality. She has made these sayings her own. Something fresh and attractive comes through when she expresses herself. It is difficult to trace the source of her charm. Jane senses that her roommate has something she doesn't have. She tries to imitate Peggy's words and gestures. She succeeds at times. The effect is not the same. Peggy has something that eludes her. Jane becomes aware of many instances in which Peggy's uniqueness shows itself unmistakably.

Peggy brings "something different" not only to dinner parties but to all she says and does. The simplest arrangement in her room bears the mark of her person. Jane begins to feel, by contrast, the shallowness of her own life. She feels irritated. Why does Peggy have something she doesn't? Peggy's poise and self-possession begin to bug her. Frustration with what she cannot be, becomes obsession. The relaxed originality of the life lived next to her is hard to bear. She feels the angry wish to destroy what she herself cannot be. But she feels powerless to do so. The destructive drive she cannot unleash on Peggy turns back upon herself. She loathes herself because she cannot be what Peggy is.

Growing vindictive, she is always ready to put a damper on Peggy's joy. But each attempt to destroy Peggy's originality proves futile. It deepens the painful awareness of the impotence of her envy. She can spoil the incidental expressions of Peggy's personality, not her personality itself. Sometimes the feeling of spite runs so deep that she feels like destroying herself. At other moments she would like to drop Peggy, to say good-by to this roommate whose self-motivated life is the source of her exasperation. The envious mood, however, has so poisoned her life that she cannot leave the source of her envy. She lives, as it were, a counter-life that needs the daily irritant of Peggy's presence to keep going. She cannot leave Peggy alone; neither can she allow her to live her life unchecked and unhampered.

Patterns of Envy

Similar patterns may develop between colleagues, mothers and daughters, fathers and sons, teachers and students, employers and employees. A person plagued by this kind of envy will pick up the faintest sign of selfhood in anyone who crosses his path. In a functional society it is easy to spot a person who is different. The man not yet assimilated as an anonymous member of the public stands out annoyingly.

Let us look again at the two girls just described. Jane is more intent on belittling Peggy's personality than on discovering and developing her own deepest self. She begrudges Peggy's self-reliance. She knows that it would be demanding to be herself, as Peggy is. To Jane the best situation would be one in which neither she nor anyone else would be an original person. To her a group of girls in which no one would be herself is infinitely preferable to a group that includes a number of girls who are themselves.

Envy of originality is malicious. Malice means that I slander the other or destroy what he has because of spite. A mother envious of a daughter who shows her own taste in fashion may maliciously undermine her self-confidence. She may tell her daughter how ridiculous she looks: "Nobody will notice you, dear, in that kind of attire." In the meantime, mother may be aware that her daughter's taste is better than her own. She herself blindly subscribes to the latest fashion simply because it is the latest. It is her daughter's originality in dress which she cannot stand. Envy prompts her malicious insinuations coated though they are with sweet concern.

Nearness and Envy

A certain nearness to the envied person seems to favor envy. Jane, tormented by envy of Peggy's originality, would probably not be envious of the originality of Mme. Curie. Some of Mme. Curie's colleagues, however, may have been devoured by the same envy Jane shows toward Peggy. Nearness is on the increase today. It is fostered by growth in population, by the false belief that we are all equal in every respect, by the functional organization of cities, towns, factories, schools, offices, and places of entertainment. We are rubbing shoulders constantly. Given such close quarters, one is more aware of the originality of the other, more pained by it, more demanding than ever that all be alike.

All societies have to cope with envy. Envy of originality, however, is more readily evoked in society today because of its tight interdependency. In his daily life a rancher feels less plagued by envy over the originality of a fellow rancher fifty miles away than a typist feels toward a fellow typist six feet away whose personality she cannot miss.

The manifestations of uniqueness which evoke envy can be simple and familiar. An extraordinary show of originality may not induce envy at all. Such originality seems to be so far out of reach that it may arouse little or no envy in the average person for whom envy has not become a way of life.

Envy arises over simple manifestations of quiet self-motivation in a person who lives next to us. Jane is upset by Peggy's spontaneous self-motivation because it is evident in the everyday things of life in which both are equally engaged. If Peggy were to show surprising originality in some specialized field—if she were, for example, a champion swimmer or a whiz in mathematics—Jane would be less annoyed.

But to be a self-reliant, sparkling self in everyday life makes one think, "I might be like her."

Perhaps the role nearness plays in envy can be traced to surroundings at home where the child may have experienced envy of originality. In childhood, originality is only in its beginning stage. It cannot yet be realized in self-motivation. The originality of childhood manifests itself mainly in spontaneity. Yet parents and children are already aware that one child is more inclined to spontaneity than others. The child's originality is not yet a threat to the grown-ups around him. His spontaneous outbursts endear him to friends and relatives. He is so cute. His antics evoke smiles of affectionate appreciation. However, brothers and sisters, who vie with the child for attention, feel that his spontaneity cuts into their share. He evokes in them not appreciation but envy.

Later in life, envious children—now grown up—may vaguely fear that the family situation will repeat itself. They live in the expectation that somebody may steal the attention they want for themselves. Even if a person hides his originality, he will not necessarily succeed in avoiding envy. In a fairly homogenized group of, let us say, soldiers, office personnel, or factory workers, each one may unconsciously do his best to be as inconspicuous as possible. Nevertheless, envy can be evoked to a surprising degree when anyone unwittingly shows his uniqueness as a person. The others suddenly become aware of what they may lack. He senses their hostility. The family situation repeats itself. Because envy between younger children in the family is an almost universal symptom, one cannot easily find a society in which the tendency to envy is totally absent.

Envy and Originality

Two aspects of originality can evoke envy. Most visible is not the unique source of original living. Envy is evoked first of all by the good things obtained occasionally by originality:

attention, promotion, status, money, or success. Only gradually may it dawn upon people that there is some connection between this success and the uniqueness that made it possible. The more I become envious of originality itself, the more I envy the person with whom I identify this quality.

Envy of originality reaches its proper meaning when the envious person recognizes originality for what it is and at the same time becomes aware of its absence in himself. He is then able to envy originality for originality's sake. Soon envy may spread from envy of successful persons to all forms of unique self-motivation in society.

The reaction of children toward a child whose originality makes them feel deprived is to demand equality. Nobody should be different. Anyone who is different threatens their share of attention and success. Inequality seems intolerable to children. They can be merciless toward anyone who stands out from the crowd. Children do not yet recognize originality as originality. They know only that the child in question is different and deprives them of attention. Children try to overcome or prevent the pain of envy by demanding the same treatment for all.

Grown-up children in the society of adults unconsciously repeat the leveling tactics of childhood. The real source of their demand for equality—envy of originality—is repressed. Leveling is done in the name of solidarity, sociability, charity, orthodoxy. This envy—carried over from childhood into adult life—hinders the development of originality in society. It also hampers the healthy growth of the envious person himself.

A society that cannot profit from the unique self-motivations of all its members is a crippled society. Our present day civilization imposes uniformity on its work and study force—a force which has become an extension of machines, computers, anonymous committees, and administrative schemes. This constant stress on uniformity often deteriorates into an implicit condemnation of any expression of spontaneity and self-motivation. In such a climate the leveling tendency of childhood, which culture should help to overcome, is strengthened instead.

Envy of Self—Envy of Others

A university professor came to visit me. He wanted a confidential talk. "My problems are rather strange," he began. "I seem to be at war with myself." I hastened to assure him that this condition was common with every man at one time or another.

"I know that," he said, "but my case seems different. I feel at war not so much with drives I cannot master but with what I cannot be. There is a war between what I cannot be at present and what I could have been if my situation would have been different. I know that sounds strange to you but please let me try to explain what I mean.

"I am a happily married man. I have a wonderful wife and four fine children. My academic life is moderately successful. But believe it or not, I am plagued by the idea of what I could have been. Family life takes a lot of energy and attention. What if I had not married? I would have had more time for study and publication. Before I married, I published a lot. I was slowly getting a name. I was invited to speak at other universities. All of this has tapered off since my marriage. At first it did not bother me. But lately I have become obsessed by that other fellow in me—that famed scholar I could have been if it were not for my family.

"I began to tell myself that this was nonsense. I should be satisfied. I was an average but well-liked teacher—no great shakes as a scholar on the national level, but respected by my colleagues and above all a man of importance to his wife and children. But that other fellow in me—that other self that I could have been—kept bothering me.

"I imagined that other self: there he was, free from family care, with ample time to read, write, and travel, enough money for books, research, and scientific trips, well groomed and rested when he appeared before an appreciative public. I became envious of that other person that I was on the road to becoming before I got married. In reaction, I began to malign his scholarship, to hate his success. I started to find fault with his imagined appearances at universities all over the country; I deprecated his trips abroad, his fancy interest in books and writing.

"But soon my predicament grew worse. I had belittled him so well that I began to believe what I was thinking. It became difficult for me to work seriously in my office. I couldn't prepare my classes well. It was more and more difficult to write an article for a scientific journal. I began to neglect my appearance. In my envious detraction of the other person in me, I came to deprecate those dimensions of life in which he would have been a success.

"I was in a dilemma. If I admitted to myself that my academic work was valuable, I felt overcome by envy for the prominent professor I could have been had I pursued my career instead of getting married. If I did not value my academic work, I would no longer feel envy for that other fellow. I could then say to myself, 'After all, he was successful in a rather "insignificant" occupation.' But the more I believed that to be true, the less I was able to give myself wholeheartedly to my academic duties.

"What is worse, I came not only to devaluate my own academic life; I began to make light of the academic zeal of others. I felt annoyed when anyone made a fuss over a person's achievement as a scholar or speaker. I discovered to my surprise that I had become as envious of the man who was praised as I was of that other self in me that I could have been."

Eying Myself with Envy

Strange as it may seem, I can be envious of myself. I can cast a spiteful eye at some dimension of my personality. I may then experience a split between myself as envious and myself as envied by myself. This split is possible because of two domains within which life may unfold itself.

The one domain is that of my daily situation. There I have to live within the limits of duties and responsibilities. The other domain is that of the style of life, labor, and leisure which I cannot maintain in my daily situation. Such possibilities—which may be real or which may only exist in my imagination—cannot be harmonized with the demands of daily life. Nevertheless such potential selves may clamor for recognition and growth. They may even develop in isolation from my harmonious unfolding in the everyday situation.

Such an "as if" mode of life may be composed of tightly interwoven fantasies, expectations, projects, and desires. At moments I may become aware of these strange forces in me. They point to values which I cannot actualize in my life as it really is. Compared with the grayness of my daily life, these unfulfilled ambitions seem to beckon me to a far more exciting and valuable existence than that which is concretely mine. Such unrealized potentials are lived for the most part in fantasy. They are not limited by the resistance daily life provides to dream. How exciting these potential modes of living seem in comparison to the harassed growth of value in my everyday surroundings!

No wonder that the real me may be inclined to look spitefully at these exciting underdeveloped lives within me. I feel envious of these beckoning strangers, the more so because I do not dare to recognize them as being also partly me. I do not dare to grant such values and possibilities the respect I should have for anything valuable in myself and others. I should be able to grant this respect—even if I must admit that in my specific life situation I cannot live these values to the full.

Self-envy is thus due to an absence of relaxed self-respect as well as to a lack of acceptance of everydayness. It may lead to repression and denial of parts of me that are truly me, even if they cannot be realized. My willful blindness

to what is really there enables these dimensions to grow in
isolation. They become loaded with unsettled feelings and
unfulfilled desires. Such dynamic tendencies may suddenly
erupt into my daily behavior, thought, and action. I experience an outbreak of inclinations which I cannot explain.
They seem strangely at odds with my personality.

Self-Envy and Envy of Others

Interwoven with self-envy is envy of others. I may meet another person who is called to live a life I myself cannot live.
Still, this life is alive in my desire, fantasy, and expectation.
Therefore I look on this person as spitefully as I look on that
part of me I have denied to myself. I feel compelled to de-
mean his role, his style, or position or even the value itself
which shows itself in his behavior. I may not understand
why I feel so uneasy or distraught when I hear people praise
him. Do they not see how insignificant his thoughts, ideas
and actions are?

If I were aware of my self-envy, I would be able to discern
the source of my irritation. Self-envy has mobilized my energy to deny and devalue my awareness of possible valuable
lives I could have lived. This denial and distortion has led
to a tension between the real me and the envied me. Respect, or an appreciative looking again at the same values
in another, threatens to break through my repression. The
praise by others of that forgotten value invites me to look
again at it with appreciation. Immediately the tension
mounts in me. More energy is frantically mobilized to fight
off this threat.

Most threatening is a person who lives the life that I would
have loved to live myself. I feel alarmed because he seems to
resurrect the desires I have buried. The attractiveness of his
life endangers the precarious truce within me. For my peace
is based on the radical dismissal of the potentially valuable
ways of life that I cannot live out. What else can I do but ex-

tend the same deprecation to these valuable modes as lived out by him? How could I keep on denying that the life I cannot live in my situation is valuable if I admit the value of the same kind of life as it is lived before my eyes by this person? The situation becomes even more frustrating to me when other people begin to express admiration for the person I envy. As I see the evidence against my devaluation mounting, my anxiety increases. Public recognition of this person's life as valuable seems to compel me to recognize the valuable potential which I could not as well develop in myself. Closing this dimension off from my awareness was my way of coping with my unfulfilled dreams and expectations. Respectful recognition now begins to unleash forces of self-doubt and insecurity.

I may rebel against my life situation. I may experience a depressive dissatisfaction with daily endeavors. Never having faced these feelings, I do not know how to deal with them. I fear that they will overwhelm me. On some level of awareness, I fear that public recognition of the value of this person may tear asunder the whole fabric of my life. I feel that I can only be saved from this calamity by responding to each increase of public praise with a reaffirmation and refinement of my envious look. I become a master in devaluation, in detecting the faults and foibles in the man I envy.

No wonder I feel compelled to find allies in this battle. I try desperately to share with others my growing envy. My alarmed defensiveness enables me to find or imagine flaws and frailties in the envied person. I gossip about him. My mounting anxiety makes me sensitive to the weak spots in friends and acquaintances with whom I want to share my envy and gossip. I play skillfully on their own needs and anxieties, evoking in them fear of the possible threat the envied person may pose to their interests. My envy becomes contagious. It corrodes the ability of others to respect and admire, to value and appreciate.

Envy, the Spoiler

Visiting friends, I meet an unexpected guest. He strikes me as a charming fellow, poised and engaging. At first I like him. Then other feelings arise. His charm makes me aware of my awkwardness. I feel clumsy, out of place. It is difficult to admit that he has something I don't. Why does he attract all the attention? His manners irk me more and more. Can't the others see through that smooth front of his? I know his kind. He seems to sense that I do not like him. He becomes self-conscious. His words come less easily. The atmosphere is strained.

I feel like the spoiler of the evening. Nobody has gained from my envious attitude, and least of all myself. It becomes impossible for me to appreciate the good in him, to learn anything from him. Worse than this, I cut myself off at that moment from my own potential for graciousness.

How different the evening could have been had I been able to keep my first interest. I could have allowed myself to feel pleased with him. I might have spoken a little less harshly than usual. I might have uncovered my own possibility for gentility. I might have sustained him in his pleasant company. I could have helped to create an agreeable atmosphere. Life for all of us that evening would have been a little less harsh, a little more humane. Now we ease toward the door, uneasily aware that things could have been better that night.

Envious Attitude, Respectful Attitude

When I think about this experience, I see more clearly the difference between what happens when my attitude is envious and when it is respectful. Envy isolates me and closes me off from the other. Appreciation—respect for the other—

brings me in tune with the goodness of my fellow man and opens me to new possibilities in myself.

The difference between these two attitudes can be seen in the way I look at the other. When I look at him in envy—though I may not call my look envious—I do not really see him. I see only what is missing in myself: in this case I see that my manner is not as attractive as his. Inwardly I begin to belittle him. I cannot appreciate in him what I do not have myself. I mock his manners, parody his behavior, poison the mood of the party. Because I never really see him, nothing he does can be good in my eyes. My first look is a look of envy.

It is interesting to note that the word "envy" comes from the Latin verb *invidere,* which means "to look askance at," "to look maliciously or spitefully into," "to cast an evil eye upon," "to envy or grudge something." Is this not exactly what I was doing? I looked askance at this man's gentleness. I cast, as it were, an evil eye upon his manners. Primitive people believed that the evil eye could spoil, sicken, or kill the other. The envious evil eye is not indifferent. It implies a spiteful look loaded with destructive feeling, a killing look, a look which, if possible, would destroy the poise of this visitor.

Once I look upon a value in the other as bad, I am unable to rejoice in this value and to make it my own insofar as this is possible. Instead I try steadfastly to deny this value. I deny it not only in the other but also in myself. Envy can lastingly blind me to certain values. It can impoverish my world of meaning and be the source of faulty perception, judgment, action.

For example, once I enviously belittle the engaging manners of a guest, I may come to reject sincere graciousness wherever I meet it. To maintain my envious views, I have to ward off any awareness of the value of that which I deny to be worthwhile. Therefore, I must keep belittling graciousness in other people. I must also fight off an appreciative awareness of gentility in myself. If I value graciousness in myself, I cannot deny the value of the same gift in others. Thus the outlook of envy becomes a source of negativity in my life.

Respect is the opposite of envy. "Respect" comes from the Latin verb *respicere* which means "to look again," "to look twice," "to pay appreciative attention," "to look benevolently," "to give the other the good eye," "to cast a good eye upon." Like envy, respect is an attitude toward people in whom certain values shine forth. If I look at this visitor with respect, I can see the value of his graciousness. I can admire and affirm it. Attracted by his gentleness, I look again and again in appreciative attention.

What lights up for me is not only this limited manifestation of gentility. The human realm of graciousness to which it points begins to come alive for me. My world of meaning deepens and expands. My humanity is nourished by my respectful look. That evening I grow in sensitivity for manifestations of gentility that may come my way. I am also more sensitive to my own possibility to grow in graciousness.

Respectful seeing carries in itself an initial movement toward my realization of the admired value. Envious seeing, on the contrary, implies a beginning project of destroying any manifestation of values upon which I look spitefully.

The Worlds of Envy and Respect

Respect and envy thus create two different worlds of meaning: a world of light and a world of darkness. Respect is a humanizing attitude, envy a dehumanizing force. The tension between respect and envy pertains to the predicament of man.

Respect leads to self-forgetful participation in value, no matter where I find it—in friend or foe. This attitude is difficult to maintain in our civilization. Our society is dominated by competition, ambition, and greed, by an intense striving for status and success. In such a society I may experience the value of the other as a threat to my own status or position. I fear that he may harm my career, diminish my popularity, or cast a shadow on my reputation, simply by outshining me. How can I admit his value as value?

In a competitive society, the envious look separates man from man. It isolates us in our private worlds, which we busily build and protect. It would be bad enough if we were closed off only from one another by envy. But envy closes us also to the mystery of value itself that nourishes our humanity. Respect would hasten our redemption from isolation. It would restore the unity of mankind and man; it would open us once again to springs of light and love. Envy darkens our world but respect illumines our despair.

Society and Originality

Certain insights can help us foster and safeguard original living in the midst of a society envious of originality. To awaken these insights is crucial, for we live in an age that wants to level us. The functional society scorns self-motivation. It tries to engulf us in public opinions, slogans, and customs. To turn us into mere public functionaries is the hidden aim of the leveling civilization.

To make life possible for millions, a rigorous organization of production and services has become necessary. Scientists and engineers devise means of mass production, consumption, employment, entertainment, and education. There is no other choice. Without organization, there would be no food, entertainment, education, transportation, health care, security, or services for most people.

The choice today is not between collective structures and structures that are not collective, between conformity and non-conformity. The choice is between being absorbed by such organizations or working effectively within them while preserving one's self-motivation.

Western man cannot survive without the mammoth organizations that support his existence. But neither can he survive as a human being without withholding something of himself from the leveling process and the public.

In the Renaissance, man ventured out from the paternalistic medieval communities to become an independent individual. He became more explicitly aware of the originality that made him a human person. In the post-Renaissance period, man was forced to devise large collective structures as conditions for survival. These discoveries cannot be undone. Modern man must live with both of them. He has to wed his newly discovered originality with collectivity, inwardness with exteriority, privacy with public life.

During the scientific and technical revolution, mankind had to develop new kinds of organizations. They were neither tribal nor paternal. Modern society has become a web of impersonal collectivities in which each person is caught. Man can lose himself in the structures of modern organization. He can relate himself to the new collectivities as he did to the tribe, the family, the medieval community —but only at the risk of making a cardinal mistake. He exposes himself to the danger of being obliterated more devastatingly as a unique person than would have been the case in the intimate communities of the past.

For the most part, I ought never to consider my company, the colleagues in my office, my political organization, or my fellow teachers as a family. If I deal with them as intimate members of my family I may be tempted to overexpose my originality. However, neither the anonymous company nor my colleagues may respect my self-motivation. What they can use for the group they will use. What is too different in me to make them feel comfortable, they may suggest that I give up, since it is not in tune with the life of the group. If I refuse to give up my originality, they may ostracize me in subtle ways. To regain acceptance I may betray a uniqueness I exposed imprudently. Precisely because I do not withhold anything from the group, I may end up without any personality of my own.

Tribes were bound together by kinship. They knew each other face to face, body to body, in the struggle for survival which was shared daily by all. They grew up together; they grew old together. Together they faced the threats of an untamed world. They shared intimately a day-to-day history.

Compared to ours, the medieval communities also were small; they consisted of town or village, the class of nobles, the clerics, or the guild of craftsmen to which one belonged. For most people it was still possible to know one another face to face, to share a common faith and ideology, to participate intimately in a shared daily history.

We find few of these characteristics in present-day society.

We are not bound together by a unity of faith or ideology. We do not share our personal histories. We do not know, as tribesmen or medieval villagers knew, the past history of each individual we meet in company, school, or city. We have become strangers to one another. Fate has packed us together in large metropolitan centers. We are not there by choice or spontaneous preference but by economic necessity. Social and economic pressures fling us together in unwieldy political movements, in unions and associations more and more difficult to oversee. The need for education herds our children into enormous school systems with countless other children who may share nothing more than age, citizenship, and the imposition of compulsory education.

Many of us do not know each other as unique persons but mainly as people with various professional, utilitarian, technical, or educational capacities. We meet each other not as persons but as competitors. The other is the one to be outdone by me. Or he is the one who will outdo me. We do not share a lively history of affective togetherness beginning in early childhood and lasting throughout life. We simply staff, along with numerous others, many of the gigantic collectivities geared to mass production. We labor monotonously, but we are cut off from the concrete visible effects of our labors. We have no immediate experience of making a meaningful impact on society by means of our organized activities.

In the future, a higher development of technique and especially of automation may counter many of the material and organizational conditions that facilitate the leveling process. In the meantime, we have to live in the present. We have to save our human originality here and now.

To resist the silent process of leveling, it is important to recognize what attitudes characterize the person engaged in this process, whether intentionally or by default. Resistance may not make you popular with most people. People who have robbed themselves of their self-motivation may resent you for it. After all, you are trying to regain in your own life what they have lost, betrayed, or never discovered in theirs. You may painfully remind them of the very thing they want to forget—their selfhood. In the leveling society this reminder is an unforgivable sin. Some may hate you for it.

Chapter Two

The Tactics of Envy

The tactics of obsessive envy we are about to describe are probably unfamiliar to most of us. Let us hope we'll never meet an obsessively envious person who tries to enlist us in his campaign. Still, it is important to consider his case. For one thing, we may not be victimized by him so easily if we are forewarned about his feelings and tactics. What is more important, the tame incidents of envy in daily life may not tell us much about envy of originality. Everyday situations may be so veiled by politeness that we fail to notice the dynamics of envy. To see them clearly, we must enlarge these dynamics beyond normal size. Looking at such magnified pictures, we begin to suspect what may happen in ourselves on a smaller scale when we give in to envy. We may also see what others may do to us when they begrudge us our uniqueness.

Where do we look when we want to see the dynamics of envy intensified? There are some people for whom envy of originality has become a way of life, indeed an obsession. Different kinds of people may become possessed by envy for different reasons. A pretentious functionary, a lazy man, a mediocre person, a fanatical conformist—these and other types may become the victim of obsessive envy. They sense the threat originality poses to their way of life. Their exceptional cases are like distorting mirrors that expose the irregularities of our features. We may deny that we are like that, but we are not so sure any more. We begin to notice tendencies we did not suspect before we were exposed to these exaggerations.

We should consider not only the case of the obsessively envious man but also that of the unusually original one. This person evokes envy precisely because of the obviousness of his originality. We should reflect on the interplay between people who are obsessively envious and those who are obviously original.

Who is obviously original? Originality as such is not obvious. Neither is self-motivation. Only to be seen are their expressions. They are more or less striking, depending on one's skill and inventiveness in self-communication and performance.

The obviously original person expresses his originality in striking achievements. A person less gifted may be more original inwardly, but he will not be known to as large a public. Nor is he as likely to draw the ire of obsessively envious people. For this reason, a better model for our consideration of the dynamics of envy as amplified out of the ordinary is the obviously original person in collision with people obsessed by envy.

Taking the exceptional case to highlight hidden dynamics of daily behavior is, of course, a common procedure. The art of caricature, the novel, the legend, the case study in pathology are examples. Few people will meet the characters portrayed in *Crime and Punishment*. Yet, we feel they are familiar to us. They show us the root of such human problems as our propensity for destruction and our seeking for forgiveness.

Obsessive Envy and Obvious Originality

The few people for whom envy of originality has become an obsession may play cleverly on the hidden envy in people who have allowed themselves to be deprived of their individuality.

I myself may be a successful man who has adapted himself well to the currents of society. I want to be kind and helpful to people; I want to meet my daily responsibilities, but my life is in a kind of rut. I have no opinions that are truly mine. I feel at ease when I share the opinion that most people happen to hold at the moment. I don't really care about the meaning of such ideas. I don't make them my own. I know that the opinion of today can get me into trouble tomorrow when another opinion may be current.

I want to feel worthwhile, to do things that deserve praise. I work hard at any enterprise I can accomplish within my self-imposed frame of conformity. As long as the task does not make demands on my repressed selfhood, I am all right. Surrounded mostly by people caught in the same trap, I gain their appreciation for my achievements. Functioning better than others may improve my position.

As an administrator, I may know every detail of the company or university machine and how it relates to other social machines in my society. I am a stickler for detail. I love committee meetings in which I can stay anonymous. I feel perfectly suited to the monotonous mood of depersonalized life.

At home I try to be a model parent, conforming to the image of parenthood promoted by radio, TV, and the Sunday papers. If the personal intrudes into my rituals of scholarship, administration, or parenthood, it strikes me as almost indecent.

I sense dimly that it is conformity to the impersonal which makes me succeed. I feel no deep envy toward those

who do as well or better than I in functional performance.
In the future I may function as well as they, perhaps even
better. I try to learn from them in order to grow day by day
beyond them in functional ingenuity.

Everything goes smoothly until my peace of mind is disturbed by the appearance of a unique man within the circle
of my life. In my superiority, I feel at ease with him at first.
He is carried away by personal feelings in administrative
meetings. He is less clever in manipulating committees. He
does not know how to emerge from painful deliberations
smelling like a rose. He has less data at his fingertips. I feel
sorry for him. The mere suggestion that I could envy such
a bumbling operator would make me laugh.

Then the unexpected happens. Some of his ideas begin to
catch on. My company tries them out. They work. One of
his publications sells well. In committee meetings the board
swings toward some of his proposals. It make me uneasy.
After all, my know-how is greater than his. To beat him
to the punch, I try for the first time in a long while to come
up with some ideas of my own. To my consternation, it seems
difficult to propose something new or daring. My repression
of originality in the sphere of the personal seems to have
affected my inventiveness on the functional level.

Worse yet, I invite this fellow to my home. My wife and
children, our friends and acquaintances, laud me for intro-
ducing such a personable guest. I go to great pains to attract
their attention to his idiosyncrasies. I cleverly join in their
praise. At the same time, I make generous excuses for those
deficiencies of his that I hope may shock my guests. To my
dismay, they assure me that they don't mind. They are in-
trigued by the way in which he meets people. It becomes
too much. I begin to suspect that in spite of my success I may
be missing something.

Vague images emerge from the past when I was more
myself, less manipulative, more of a creative human being.
Did I perhaps lose my grip? This is too threatening to con-

template. I slam the door on such memories. But the feelings return. I angrily denounce and devalue the original self in me that tries to emerge. I tell myself that people are wrong to be taken in by this phony who is less of a storehouse of information than I. I look eagerly for flaws in his so-called creative contributions. In the field of knowledge they *must* be unsubstantiated, in the field of administration they *must* be at odds with the facts, in the field of religion they *must* be heretical.

I begin cautiously to express my discomfort and suspicion. I might say, "I feel dubious about our friend. That kind of person tends to be somewhat unbalanced. One should be careful where such people are concerned." Careful to express my envy modestly, I conceal its intensity. Vehement feelings are frowned upon in polite society. So I project the image of a wise, balanced person. Talking excitedly, I might evoke suspicion. Others might jump to the conclusion that I was prejudiced. I want them to feel that I am moved simply by common sense, by concern for the public interest. I can discredit the other more effectively when I show temperance.

I may say something like this: "Personally I have nothing against him. It's refreshing to hear new ideas. Of course, one must always be careful with that kind of person." When I have established myself in the minds of my audience as a reasonable fellow, I can go further: "I like him, but there is *something* about him that makes me uneasy."

First I present an image of sense and mitigation. My listener, a "regular guy," appreciates moderation. Then I pass along a feeling of suspicion. It may catch on like a contagious disease. I suggest discreetly that *something* is wrong with this fellow. Nobody knows what. But I hope that this suggestion may be enough to evoke a vague uneasiness.

Now I am ripe bait for the expert who has made the leveling of the self-motivated person his mission in life. He will sense my anxiety, my discomfort. He soon sneaks up to me.

Confidentially he speaks to me about the danger this well-meaning person presents to our company and community. He realizes, of course, that most people in their goodness and simplicity do not suspect the threat he presents to them. But he knew from the beginning that I, in my position, with my success, with my discernment and balanced judgment, would see through him. Here at least is one man of vision who realizes the same thing I have already begun to suspect.

Before knowing what happens, I am enlisted in his campaign against the original man. He tells me about other dignitaries higher than I with whom he has spoken. They share my concern. It feels good to be on the side of such men. It restores my self-respect. Supported by like-minded fellows, I feel obliged to temper the rash enthusiasm of my misguided colleagues, employees, superiors, friends, and family. I assure them that I myself was taken in at first by this charming fellow. But what is my judgment against the judgment of all these higher-ups? I discover to my delight that many of those who admired our original friend also, of late, have developed the same uneasy feelings about him. The unfortunate fellow took over some of the deference they felt entitled to. They are relieved to find such noble reasons to cut this upstart down to size.

My new acquaintance generously spends his time enlightening people about the dangers posed by this spontaneous fellow. He begins to work on some of my more influential friends. He assures me we need not worry about people in lesser positions. We have to protect them against perils they cannot fathom themselves. They are good listeners though, for they are eager to be in with those of us who have made it in this society. The majority will gladly go along with us. At the right moment they may be turned into a symbolic lynching mob. Real lynching is out of the question nowadays. Besides, the fellow who was lynched in the past died quickly. This pretentious climber will be made to suffer daily from the gradual destruction of his reputation and career.

Thus the first class of people to become the tools of those who have made the leveling of original persons a life project are usually successful, impersonal men, who possess everything but the spark of originality. The man who seeks to destroy self-motivated people plays on the anxiety evoked in them whenever a person true to himself enters their life.

Tactics of the Envious Man

A man possessed by envy usually operates behind the scenes. He undermines the self-motivated person, not by legal means or public discussion. Rather he insinuates. He ridicules. He makes suspect.

He would fail within the framework of legal structures or open debate. He turns to camouflage tactics instead. He cleverly goes around the codes and structures of society. His tactic is to corrupt the sentiments of influential men. When the creative person makes a mistake, the envious man is on the alert to draw attention to this fact. He has developed a "sixth sense" for spotting any fault in a self-motivated person. He tries to trick him. He is delighted when he gets him to say something in excitement that can be used against him. He takes it out of context and displays his gossipy gem at parties and social gatherings. He quotes the incident persistently, savoring each word that might make the original man look bad in the eyes of others. Every time he distorts the story a little more. He is clever enough to disguise his damaging information as good-natured, anecdotal banter so as not to endanger his own reputation. His story gladdens and amuses his listeners, many of whom have no lost love for people who choose to be themselves.

The fact that the original person is not like other people arouses the indignation of the envious man. What he disapproves of—his uniqueness, originality, self-motivation—he disapproves of not only in him but in all people, including himself.

He aims blindly at leveling all that is unique about this person's life. What he hates is not this man's reputation or goals. His unique self is the target. His undaunted selfhood —the source of his creative expression and fresh perception— is what threatens the man obsessed by envy of originality. He will go to any length to destroy an envied person. If possible, he will resort to imprisonment, slander, censorship, burning at the stake, or any other kind of symbolic or real killing.

The goal of a life dominated by envy is the death of the original person. To be sure, the envious man does not demand this openly. He does not even know that he wants it. The wish for the creative man's demise is expressed symbolically in his attempt to destroy this person's reputation. Reputation is the way a person lives in the minds and hearts of people. Man's most vulnerable spot is his image in the consciousness of others. So the envious man sets out to break down the respect he finds in influential people for a self-motivated person.

Symbolic sacrifice of the unique person is justified by the rationalization that it serves the common good. It is better that one person dies than that all people perish. Symbolic murders are perpetrated in good conscience. The passionately anti-original person feels that it is his mission to do away with innovators and creative thinkers. Gossip and slander become his main weapons. He finds in them a way of escaping awareness of his own murderous wishes while still giving in to them. He imagines himself a charismatic figure, delegated by fate to safeguard the common good.

The scene of symbolic assassination may assume ritualistic proportions, not unlike human sacrifice in certain cultures. It was often the outstanding person who was designated to die as an offering to the gods. Envy may have influenced the selection. The tribe could admit the assets of its victims, at the same time eliminating him without embarrassment. Should not only the best be offered to the gods? By destroying the outstanding person ritually, the tribe escaped the self-torture of envy.

The immolation enabled them to preserve their capacity for admiration. They did not have to deny the valuable qualities of their victim. On the contrary, his gifts made him more worthy as a sacrifice. In some cases the tribe carried its envy over to the gods. The gods were envious of gifted people. To placate them they had to be slain ritually.

Religious justifications for the assassination of prominent people are not alien to contemporary society. Beneath the veneer of modern man still lurks the primitive. An envious person today may justify his symbolic immolation of original people with justifications that remind us of our tribal past. He may carry his own envy over to a god, coating the sacrificial process with religious significance. He may say that his god suffers from the originality of the self-motivated person, which is really pride and conceit. The god of justice looks with a spiteful eye on the original person. He is a scandal and temptation to the people of God. He, the well-balanced, unassuming conformist—not wise with the wisdom of this world but with the wisdom of the beyond—is called in his unworthiness to be the humble inquisitor, the holy hangman of the self-motivated person.

Sometimes slanderous words and gestures take on a ritualistic aura. They are expressed in unctuous conviction. The voice sinks to a confidential whisper. The face features shocked indignation about the outrageous words and actions of the self-motivated man. Listeners are quickly drawn into the atmosphere of righteous indignation. They feel holy outrage that this fellow dared to offend the gods by the hubris of his creativity. Their voices become hushed; their tone conspiratorial. Together they immolate the envied person symbolically, out of love for God and the public good. Meanwhile, they reassure each other that this sacrifice is sacred. They repeat in a variety of ways that it is their duty to silence the self-motivated upstart in their community, painful as this may be. At the end of their ceremony, they may feel the peace and satisfaction that comes after a duty well done, a ritual well performed.

Their victim, in the meantime, may involve himself in some engrossing enterprise in service of others. Intensely occupied, he minds his own business. He pays no attention to the tactics of envious schemers. Strategically, he should spend more time at social gatherings and committee meetings, in cafeterias and at parties. Perhaps he could then undo the evil image of himself that his detractors are building up.

However, to fight scheming with more scheming would destroy him as a person. Trying to meet his opponent on his own ground would endanger his integrity. His major concern would have to be with what influential people are whispering about him rather than with what he really is. If he tried to answer all the rumors spread around, he would lose his equanimity. His attention would run in diverse directions, chasing after rumors, for there is no plan or reason to gossip. He would lose his capacity for respect and admiration. And, if that were to happen, then the envious man would win in an ultimate sense: he would have perverted the respectful person by infecting him with his own disease.

Neither would it do much good to the envied man to give up a successful enterprise to placate the envy of those around him. He may cherish the illusion that their spiteful objections are evoked by so-called pernicious features of his current pursuit. But envy of originality is not aroused by this or that engagement. The uniqueness of the person himself is at stake. To satisfy his detractors, the creative man shifts to a modest, less controversial undertaking. But that one also evokes criticism. Changing from project to project may finally force him to realize that he could only please his opponents were he to vanish from the face of the earth. Nothing may have been wrong with his work. The only thing wrong was himself. His unique motivation brought something to his activities that those around him could not endure. He committed the unforgivable sin in an equalized society—that of being himself.

Beyond threatened influential men there is another ready audience to be aroused by the man possessed by envy: people who love to impersonate men of importance. Neither passionately envious nor personally resourceful, they cherish few opinions or feelings of their own. They do not scorn self-motivated people, but neither do they respect them. They would not harm them but neither would they say a word to protect their reputation or position. Since it seems important to appear to be something, they cheerfully repeat the important-sounding phrases uttered by persons who carry weight.

The few for whom the destruction of originality has become a way of life may succeed in tricking weighty people into mumbling frightened phrases about annoying upstarts. Ambitious imitators are eager to repeat their words. They love to parrot important people. They do not mean to harm the self-motivated person. They seek only some affirmation of themselves by their faithful parroting of opinions that seem to be "in" at the moment.

Such persons change with the times. To borrow the latest opinion about some self-motivated person is like sitting in the booing section of the house. They pick up the chant that some unique fellow is a cheat and a scandal. They pretend to protect society against impending disaster. They even mimic the excitement with which these ponderous pronouncements are uttered. That pretense of shocked indignation makes them feel for a moment that they are coming to life. They are a ready troupe for any leveling project.

Soon the instigator succeeds in turning men of influence and their imitators against original people around them. The time is ripe for symbolic execution. It is easy to enlist

the crowd now. Dormant in the population at large is a latent
envy of all those whose success makes them feel under-
privileged. Usually the mass man does not have a chance to
harm outstanding persons. The thought of leveling may not
even occur to him. This situation changes when a public
execution is pending. The mob smells blood. Bodily execution is no longer feasible. Symbolic execution takes its place.
The moment a self-motivated man begins to lose his name
and position, one can sense the thinly disguised glee of many
mass men, the indifference of others who could not care less
that this ambitious fellow got what he deserved. Without the
co-operation of all these people, the agitator against self-
motivated persons would not be able to succeed in his leveling tactics.

Irritation Evoked by the Obviously Original Man

The original person reminds people of a life that might have
been theirs had they not crippled their potential for creative
living. Facing the self-motivated man, the impersonal one
feels exposed. He feels called upon to be himself. His
anonymity is threatened. For an anxious moment, he feels
isolated from the daily source of his thought and movement:
the anonymous public.

Many people, while tolerating a hierarchy of administrative and professional positions, insist that they be well de-
fined and predictable. They like to believe, in principle if
not in fact, that each one of them could be cast into each
one of these social roles if their education gave them the
necessary preparation. They hate to be reminded of the inequality between people in the realm of originality, talent,
and possibility. They prefer the illusion that there are only
interchangeable positions: every man can assume them
when a vacancy arises, provided he has the professional
qualifications.

Even so, a person in an advantageous administrative or

professional position may evoke envy though he is not particularly original. We could call this an "envy of position." Such envy differs from the envy of selfhood, which may arise when an original man appears on the scene.

The original person deviates too obviously from the unwritten rule that nobody is irreplaceable. He may be replaceable in his function. He is clearly irreplaceable as a person. Many people envision the model society as a flawless machine. Each homogenized part should be replaceable by any other. All that matters is that the person concerned have the right training. In their minds a man serves the collectivity best by homogenizing himself so completely that he is always available to replace any missing piece of equipment, with no consideration for his own motivation, talent, and temperament.

While this omni-availability is impossible, it may be exalted as an ideal. This ideal demands that each man forfeit his potential for personal life. The self-motivated person stands out as an annoying obstacle to its realization. He reminds people of the desire to be themselves. They have to contain this desire. His presence threatens to awaken it. He evokes embarrassment, guilt, shame, and anger. Were the message of his life to come through, the dormant volcano on which the leveling society is built might erupt.

Social Position of the Self-Motivated Man

The social position of a self-motivated man may be hazardous. Fellow workers may threaten his chances for promotion. They distrust people like him. His position may be especially in jeopardy when an envious man becomes his superior. The latter feels supported in his leveling tactics by the latent envy of other staff members and employees. He realizes that he can make almost any move against the envied man. He will probably be applauded in his efforts by most of the people around him.

The boss himself may have climbed the ladder of success by slavish compliance with people who had already made it. Servility to the system put him on top of the self-motivated man he secretly envies and fears. Now this man depends on him for his means of subsistence. The superior watches his anxious attempts to please him, the awkward way he tries to hide his ideas and feelings—not out of personal weakness but out of concern for his family.

All of this elates the supervisor. The fear he evokes in the self-motivated man gives him a sense of power. This man's fate rests in his hands. Caution and flattery will not cure the envy of this boss. The original man should never expect to win the battle for acceptance. He may pretend that he is a regular guy—not worthy of the least bit of envy—but to no avail. No matter how he tries to hide it, it's clear that here is one who is still his own man. It is only the weakness of his social position that moves him to displays of subjugation.

To respect his subordinate in his selfhood would imply a revolution in the superior. It would open his eyes not only to the uniqueness of this employee but to his own uniqueness as well. This awareness could force a change in his values, attitudes, and defenses. But at the same time this change would imply the willingness to risk his status in the leveling community.

Envious Look, Respectful Look

A life of leveling envy thrives in a climate of suspicion and condemnation. Envy excludes the appreciative look of respect. Envy's refusal to "look again" makes the condemnation of the original man inflexible and absolute.

The respectful person, by contrast, experiences his view as tentative. His mind is open to new perspectives. Valuable sides of the other's personality may reveal themselves. They cast doubt on his former opinion. They invite him to look again. The respectful person never sees clearly where his openness may lead him. New insights constantly light up for him. He hesitates before he passes judgment.

The envious look of the impersonal man, on the contrary, is a look of certitude. He prides himself on the unshakability of his opinions. He seeks to have them confirmed by "facts" and "common sense." He does not look twice at the person he chides. What he looks for are words and incidents that justify his disapproval. He dislikes people who are moved by self-motivation. They are unpredictable. They threaten the familiar scheme of things.

The envious man cannot risk uncovering the streak of originality he has buried in himself. Under his ponderous self-assurance, waiting to be tapped, is a hidden source of spontaneity. Its discovery could lead him to a new style of life. But to follow the call of his unique self would imply not figuring himself out once and for all.

Willful Mediocrity and Anti-Originality

The impersonal man may claim that he has no illusions about his own capacities. He considers himself an average fellow, a modest functionary who performs his duties reasonably well, a nice guy in no way different from the other nice guys around him. By no means does this man feel embarrassed by the drabness of his life. He is proud of it. He declares just a bit too strongly that he is delighted to be that way. However impersonal his life already is, he takes every precaution to make it even more so. He fears attracting attention to his self-motivations, if he has any left. He sticks to those like him who are mainly moved by public opinion, living in compliance with one or the other set of successful functionaries. He embraces with relief their style of life, their thoughts and feelings. In his envious attempt to level original people, he exalts conformity as such. For him, impersonal performance within academic, economic, or political organizations should not allow any intrusion of inwardness or personal concern.

The impersonal man feels that his public sense and practical ingenuity absolve him from any obligation to think or question on a personal level. This kind of "common sense" frees him from having to appropriate personally any value that might motivate him uniquely.

Common Sense and Common Wisdom

When in everyday life I say, "He has common sense," it usually means that one is a sensible person. However, "common sense" for a mediocre functionary, fearful of personal thought, may have a special meaning. "Public sense" would be a better word for it.

We must distinguish this kind of "common sense" from "common wisdom." Common wisdom may be the gift of simple people who will never be creative in an unusual way. The simple man, who has not betrayed his humanity, will remain faithful to his own modest self. He is wise enough to recognize that his life should be enlightened by the wisdom of mankind. He lives in respect for the values discovered by humanity.

Because respect permeates his life, he is creative. What he creates is not necessarily a specific thing. Human creativity aims at something more fundamental. His creativity is a penetration into the mystery of value. Value lies hidden in events and things, in the words, acts, and customs of people. The simple man is always open to hidden values. He senses them in the wisdom and traditions of generations. He does not copy them. He tries to live them personally. In this sense his openness for value makes him creative. As a human person, he is superior to a learned man who would choose to remain mediocre as a human being. The simple self-motivated man may be as superior to him as the person whose self-motivation shows itself in striking expression. His capacity for thought, speech, and action, however, is limited. He does not easily catch the attention of others. But sometimes, in an emergency situation, for instance, his hidden greatness may come to the fore. In contrast to his courage, the envious mediocre man may desert the ship. When valueless men have fled, simple people in faithfulness to values may stay behind to perform heroic deeds.

Perversion of Attitudes and Action by Envy of Selfhood

Envy of selfhood cannot be confined to one dimension of the envied person or to one attitude of the man possessed by envy. It spills over into other attitudes. Affability may be tainted by an all-pervading envy of the unique. Kind acceptance of another may be marred by a hidden condition: in no way must he reveal himself as a true person with unique motivations. The envious person may overflow with joviality as long as the other consents not to be himself.

Envy perverts human actions in the same way as it perverts human attitudes. If an envious schemer adheres to some religion, he may abuse the tenets and structures of his church to level others. In past history he might have been a supporter of violent state-enforced inquisition in the hope that it could be abused to detect and control self-motivated people. In modern times he might promote fact-finding committees if they can be composed of conformists like himself, consumed by the same scorn of what is unique.

The poison of envy spreads to all acts and attitudes. No self-motivated man for long escapes the venom of its sting. Obsessive envy contaminates all judgments. To the warped, envious mind, each endeavor of the original person—a talk he gives, a book he writes, a solution he proposes—is suspect. Obsessive envy may see faults, sinister meanings, heresies, and dangers in such ventures, even if they are not really there.

As the envious man understands it, the obviously original person pollutes everything he says and does. He contaminates the language he speaks, the journals he contributes to, the audiences he addresses, the students to whom he lectures, the congregations to which he preaches.

No fact-finding committee may be able to establish a link between the envied person and the evil imputed to him. But an envious fellow will fall back on his "common sense," on his sensitivity for the public interest; it warns him of the dangerous influence of the self-motivated person.

From the factual point of view, an envied speaker or teacher can prove that he did not say the things attributed to him. Legally he is untouchable. But, the envious person adds in the same breath, precisely behind this front of decency lurks the evil. Triumphantly he brings to the fore what others miss: the fact that it is impossible to get the original person convicted proves his untrustworthiness. His perversion leads him to do the wrong thing under all circumstances and, at the same time, to cover it up so cleverly that no one can convict him legally.

Envy and Renewal of Society

Another type of person obsessed by envy may be the fanatical conformist. Mere conformity is the refusal to live a life that is personally motivated. The conformist may wish to be anything—a regular fellow, a plain Joe, a perfect functionary, a clever operator, a famed scholar—anything but a self-motivated person. He may want to learn everything, to meet everyone, to hold every position, but he stubbornly refuses to be the origin of motivations that are at odds with those of the public. He is careful that nothing touches the core of his humanity, where he is called to be the origin of his own world of meaning and motivation.

A conformist obsessed by envy of originality lives in fear. He is afraid of himself, of his uniqueness, of the burden of responsibility that recognition of his selfhood may place upon him. His envy of original people is not simply an opinion but a way of life. It is an obsession that makes him unimaginative, inflexible, and impervious—not only in regard to his attitude toward the self-motivated person but in regard to all views and attitudes that threaten conformity in society.

To him, the problem-free society will emerge at the moment everyone is reduced to a blissful state of anonymity. Harmony will prevail once all self-motivated people have been leveled out or eliminated. Never does it strike him that society should at all times be renewed in a personal sense.

For him renewal of community is not the question; the real question is how to perfect the impersonal community we already have. This well-organized society would be capable of pushing forward were it not for the annoying disturbances caused by people who are always coming up with something new.

In pursuit of this ideal society, the conformist aspires to enlist the collaboration of all men of good will. He defines in advance who these men will be. The original man is necessarily excluded: he is a man of incurable bad will. Original sin in the theological sense can be washed away, but the original sin of originality cannot be erased.

The explanation of unpleasant events becomes easy for a conformist possessed by envy. Everything wrong is due to the sin of self-motivation. Everything would be fine if everyone were leveled out. He has no time to think about his community constructively. He is too busy watching any move a self-motivated man may make. He does not want to lose his precious hours in the pursuit of personal renewal. If something has to be done to improve society, he tells himself it can be done by other good-willed impersonal men who will come after him. By his cleaning-up operation, he is preparing the way for them. His business is to unmask creative troublemakers, to denounce and expose them.

Revolution and the Original Man

In periods of normality, self-motivated persons may stay in the background, wary of evoking the wrath of envious people. Their attitude may change in times of upheaval.

Revolution breaks down familiar patterns of life. The impersonal man lived by them. He was not conspicuous. He did not have to make choices concerning his personal stand. Society did that for him. Revolution catches him unaware. He loses his grip on social life, but not for long. He soon guesses which way the wind blows, what the new patterns of conformity will be.

The self-motivated man is less fortunate. Revolution or no revolution, he remains a uniquely responsible person. In the beginning of the revolution, he may be hailed as an ally, praised because of his lack of identification with the status quo. Though the revolution may succeed in creating a new kind of life, the self-motivated person remains himself. He is not wholly identifiable with the new state of affairs. It is just as impossible for him to level himself out in terms of the new patterns of conformity as it was for him to do so in regard to former styles of living.

Impersonal men have no trouble. They adapt easily to the new stereotypes. Having no noticeable selfhood, they have nothing to lose. In the beginning of the revolution, some self-motivated people may delude themselves into thinking that the interruption of conformity is a lasting event. They expose their self-motivation in an unguarded way. Their spontaneous self-expression is admired during the revolt. After the victory, it may prove embarrassing.

Any originality after a revolution may cast doubt on the new orthodoxy. Creative difference may soon be indicated as counterrevolution or revisionism. The impersonal man sees his chance. He puts himself at the disposal of the new

Establishment; he too clamors for the destruction of the man who remains himself.

This situation is just another way of showing that an obviously original person can rarely claim victory; he can only survive. In times of revolution, however, he may let his guard down. As a result, at the end of a revolutionary period, he may neither win nor survive. The unguarded exposition of his selfhood makes him suspect in the eyes of the new Establishment. It takes a dim view of conspicuous originality.

Envy and Collegiality

Many communities today in neighborhood and town, in school and business, in social work and charitable enterprise, are becoming collegial. Democracy, so to speak, is spreading downward. The democracy that has been realized on a national level is now being tried in countless small groups that make up our democratic society. What the champion for equality was in political life, the collegial man tries to be in school, church, or neighborhood. Collegiality has for him the same sacred ring that political equality had for those who fought for human rights in revolutionary times. Just as they demanded an equal vote for all, so the collegial man hopes to reform each small community by allowing everyone an equal say in its administration. Some go even further. They want the collegial community to have a say in the personal life of each one of its members—of course, for their own good and that of the community.

At first sight, collegiality seems an ideal climate for the free unfolding of the self-motivated person. He need no longer feel compelled to comply with the cramping views of a few impersonal people who happen to be in command. The prospect of freedom delights him. The slogans of those who call for collegiality may beguile him. He hears splendid tales about the ruling of the community by the community.

Within the collegial atmosphere, everyone will be encouraged to become the origin of his own life. The result will be a community of increasingly self-motivated people. They will foster mutual respect. To believe the myth of collegiality, each collegial man will be delighted when someone is more original and successful than he. Collegial togetherness will mark the beginning of a new and better world.

In reality, things are not necessarily that good in the collegial community. In some instances, such communities may turn out to be more leveling than those of a more traditional sort. A person who tries to be himself may be flattened out more effectively than before. It all seems to hinge on the image that a collegial man has of community and the person. If that image of the person is functional, sterile, and pragmatic, true collegiality is not likely to be achieved. Collegiality is one way of functioning in a community. Whether this means—neutral in itself—will be used well depends on the idea of the person in light of which collegiality is exercised. Collegiality may foster community life when inspired and limited by respect for the person as person. It can be pernicious when it starts from the implicit presupposition that persons are community "things."

A man moved mainly by the reflexes of the public may seize on collegiality as a way of keeping self-motivated people in line. When he swings the majority to his side, he can carry out his leveling project. For him, community is collectivity: a collection of regular fellows who should all feel the same, act the same, be the same.

Thus the self-motivated man and the impersonal one may both proclaim the beauty of collegiality without realizing that they do not have the same goal in mind. If the creative person claims that collegiality will leave room for everyone's opinion, the impersonal one may wholeheartedly agree with him. But they do not mean the same.

The original man means that every person may be self-motivated differently. He feels that this difference in self-motivation can be the origin of each one's unique way of life and thought. Collegiality should respect and promote this difference as long as it is compatible with the essential demands of the common life. The original person feels that the community profits to the degree that it allows its members to be their best selves.

To the impersonal man, a community is a collection of individuals who are essentially the same. All can be asked without imposition to execute the same functions and attend the same sessions—namely, those the majority feels will make life easier and more compatible with the needs of the average fellow in the group. What the collectivity engages in, what it allows a member to be or not to be, will often be determined by the average men of the community who may form the solid majority. At times such men may want to protect themselves against guilt and inferiority feelings, against the pain of envy evoked by self-motivated people, against the pursuit of excellence, against deviations from prevalent public opinions. They may propose plans of prudent action, to which all must conform generously. Collegiality implies, of course, that a few mavericks may freely say that they do not like what is proposed; the majority will vote them down anyway.

The self-motivated man has less recourse than ever. It is difficult to fight against a measure voted in by the group as a whole, especially when the group has allowed one to have his say. In some cases the tyranny of the average opinion can be exceedingly subtle. The so-called collegial community may proclaim that it makes "consensus" its ideal. Once this ideal is proposed, people can be made to feel guilty and wayward if they do not admit that the average opinion is the best one, even if a measure voted in would drastically diminish the practical conditions for privacy and for living their own life personally.

To the impersonal type of collegial man, an individual is a statistical average of traits all members possess. Anything beyond the usual in personal value is superfluous, eccentric, an affront to the common life. His defense of each member's equal rights is in reality a defense of each member as an average functional man who may have his say within the limits of the "common sense" and public opinion of the group. The opinion of an individual should merely be an insignificant variation of the average feelings of the community.

True collegiality, however, is the art of promoting each person in his uniqueness within the limits of a common life or task. Community is people. People are called to be self-motivated. Self-motivation makes for differences. One should thus never decide what a community should do before considering concretely the people who make up the community, their qualifications and inclinations. Collegiality is a communal style of respect for personal differences.

Collegiality enlightened by respect can never mean the suppression of someone's personal calling by a vocal majority. Collegiality mellowed and illumined by respect is marked by sensitive concern for what the call of each member may be. Such patient sensitivity demands detachment from envy when a person's self-realization happens to entail benefits unavailable to others not similarly gifted—detachment from one's limited judgment when he realizes that by endowment, background, and education he is not capable of wholly understanding why some person must do what he does the way he does it.

Collegiality of men who are humble and detached is a blessing. Collegiality without respect and humility can be hell. The more the members of a collegial community are liberated from blind fascination with their own ideas or with the glorious plans of their organization, the more they may foster self-motivation in each individual. Collegiality should develop the art of creating projects and structures which give each person a reasonable scope of possibilities in which to realize his originality, without jeopardizing the minimum requirements for a certain unity.

The man whose view of collegiality is inauthentic is prone to believe that upon entrance into a community one can sever a member from his selfhood, his personal history, religion, world view, specific talents, and interests. In this man's view, the individual is plunged into a common enterprise as a solitary particle no different from any other. Nothing is to be left to the person but to be a well-functioning cog in the machinery of collegial collectivity.

There is a tinge of anti-originality in many a collegial enthusiast in spite of all his protests to the contrary. He may feel hostile to the original man who refuses to surrender his self-motivation. He betrays his frustration when he indulgently declares: "The only thing I have against this fellow is his lack of community spirit."

While the impersonal type of collegial man may brim with good will and generosity, he may prove useless in the defense of the self-motivated person. He is naïvely proud of being open to all sides. He suavely avoids any conflict that may disrupt what he calls peace, love, and brotherhood. He is a professional peacemaker, inclined to appease the anti-original loudmouth. He wants to reconcile him. The original man is always the victim of this sentimental desire for brotherhood. The impersonal collegial man professes moderation. He is tolerant by vocation. He is even snobbish about his tolerance, extending it by preference to loud and vulgar people he secretly fears. His obsequious "understanding" gives them the extra room they may need to destroy the conditions for another's self-motivated life.

Rather than feeling consoled, the original man may feel endangered when an enterprise becomes collegial. Such an undertaking may not necessarily value unique dedication, personal growth, individual dignity. It may be primarily concerned about feelings and opinions cherished by colleagues and the public. I am successful to the degree that I am able to please my boss and my colleagues; I am liked when I make them feel good, when I do not evoke feelings of guilt, inferiority, or envy. Self-motivation is bad news in this atmosphere.

Not only the communities that make up society but society as a whole could become collegial. Then the conformistic crowd may take over. In that case, only those who please the crowd will be promoted. It becomes necessary to praise, seduce, and entertain both the public and one's colleagues in daily life. I must work especially on those people who are on the committees that dominate and structure the collegial society. Countless ceremonies have to be performed in order to attract confidence and gain approval. Socializing and back-slapping may become more conducive to promotion or survival than production, study, thought, and initiative. Of course, people who are not living on the level of human originality may also be productive, studious, and inventive. However, the problem facing the man who is loyal to himself is that he permeates the use of these same abilities with his self-motivations; his talents are the specific means in and through which he makes his latent originality actual.

In a leveling collegial collectivity, it may not be the finest human being who reaches the pinnacle of success and status. It is for the best crowd pleaser, for the obvious conformist, the smooth talker, that the highest positions and greatest economic compensations may be reserved.

The obviously original person may try to show that he too is in favor of adaptability and regular fellowship, that he does not want to rock the boat, that he admires those who symbolize success in his society. In this attempt, however, he usually lags behind the impersonal man. Unlike him he has to cope with the reputation that he is an original character to begin with and not a regular fellow. This reputation was imposed upon him when he inadvertently betrayed his self-motivation. From that moment on, he was a marked man. He cannot free himself from his bad name. No matter what he does, he is not allowed to forget that he is not really one of the "trustworthy regular guys." This is the highest accolade an impersonal collegial community can bestow on those who level themselves as human beings. They are proud to keep the machinery of the homogenized collectivity running smoothly. Some of them pollute their surroundings with a sticky, suffocating atmosphere of "brotherhood," "peace," and "loving encounter," which in reality may not show true respect for the uniqueness of the person.

Concluding Remarks

Purposely we have presented in this chapter rare situations of obsessive envy and conspicuous originality not often encountered in daily life. Our aim was to awaken recognition of implicit tendencies of envy in ourselves as well as recognition of those situations in which envy may be easily aroused. We may never face such extreme forms of envy. But we may at least recognize the minute embryonic appearances of similar dynamics in ourselves and others. And, if ever the obsessive case crosses our path, we know what to expect.

Armed with this new sensitivity, we can now look more closely at some other appearances of envy and suggest ways in which we ought to deal with them. Then we will be ready to take a closer look at originality and self-motivation in their usual appearances and at the general problems that contemporary life poses to original living.

Chapter Three

Dealing
with Envy

Destructive traits are readily deplored in others, rarely recognized in myself. While not obsessively envious, I may be prone to envy at various times. Envy can affect my fantasies, thoughts, and feelings, without my even being aware of it.

I may be afraid to admit to envy because it makes me feel inferior and guilty and I do not know how to handle such feelings. They scare me. Too frightened to face envy in myself, I prefer to regard it as something outside of me. I can then sit back, relax, and scrutinize this interesting phenomenon with detached curiosity, seeing it in the rest of mankind but not in myself. Or I may ascribe envy to one person I already happen to dislike. I enshrine all envy in him. Unfortunately, as long as I see envy only in other people, I can neither gain in self-insight nor improve my relations with others.

For similar reasons I may overlook envy in the people around me. Not being an obviously original person, the envy I arouse in loved ones, friends, colleagues, and companions is likely to be less violent and therefore more difficult to spot. I may be afraid to face the fact that each one of my acquaintances could envy my self-unfolding, reputation, happiness, career; that envy could lower my neighbor's appreciation of my best endeavors, diminish my family's love and care for me, poison my friendships, and make colleagues more harmful than helpful. To keep this fear down, I simply choose to ignore their envy of me. In the meantime, an envious boss, friend, fiancée, or spouse may belittle me in subtle ways, undermine my reputation with "innocent" jokes and sly hints, or impute to my efforts self-centered designs. On another occasion, I may not protest, even inwardly, when a well-meaning counselor or teacher—out of unconscious envy—gives me wrong advice, convinced that he is saving my future.

When I ignore the possibility of envy in people who claim to help me or in those who are close to me, I increase its potentially destructive power over me. It is wiser to ask in what way envy can affect the attitudes and actions of others toward me. Then I can deal with it more effectively.

Reflecting on envy should help me to discover my own envy and the envy of others insofar as it affects me. Clarifying these two dimensions should better enable me to cope with envy in my life. When I feel and admit envy in myself, I may not only improve myself but also learn to deal with the same affliction in others. Then when I am the target of envy, I know from my own experience what is eating away at the person who envies me. I become vigilant in a reasonable and relaxed way to what might ignite this feeling in him unnecessarily.

Such compassion may not cure the pain of envy in others or stem their tactics against me. It may not prevent the eventual destruction of my work and reputation. But enlightened compassion does soften the tension. Compassion is not passivity. It is a source of thought and action which, in an understanding way, takes into account the envious leanings of those around me.

Compassion, however, does not mean that I should be blind to envious schemes in regard to my person and endeavors. Empathy alone could make me a naïve victim of plots and intrigues. If I do not resist envious tactics which could be overcome, I might become an accomplice to the destruction of my own reputation or work. To escape loneliness and to court acceptance, I might comply with the envious demands of my husband, wife, sweetheart, superior, colleague, or friend. In this way, I allow their envy to paralyze my initiative as a person. On the other hand, I must be cautious not to misinterpret as envious a reasonable demand that merely conflicts with self-centered interests of my own.

An original man whose originality reveals itself in exceptional performance may be plagued by envy to the last day of his life. It may silence his voice, halt his activities, darken his reputation. Still, his perseverance may delay the victory of envy. Before he has to face the moment of defeat, he may accomplish something of value that expresses not only his skill, zeal, and talent but in and through these his personal values and self-motivations. Even this respite may not be granted to him, however. The triumph of envy may be too swift. Still, his attempt has not been in vain. His persistence will be a light for some. His example reminds them to be faithful to their own initiatives in spite of detraction. Inspired by his courage, they may stand up in turn, willing to be counted.

When the tactics of envy endanger the effectiveness of my life and work, I should take them seriously and deal with them wisely. I may be tempted to give up resistance simply because I want so much to be in with the gang. In their amicable suggestions I refuse to recognize the assault on what is best in me. They may never say directly that they do not want me to be different. They honestly may not know how much they resent my expression of self-motivation in daily life. The poison of their envy can be tucked away in attractive packages at the sight of which I am supposed to light up with delight. Some of these wrappings are good fellowship, care for my health, concern for my sanity, virtue, good name. The more poisonous the content, the lovelier the wrapping is likely to be. A trick envious people may use is to enlist me in various enterprises ill-suited to my personality or in countless committee meetings which cut unnecessarily into the time I need to pursue projects for the human community more in keeping with my capacities.

The wise man is alert when abundant care begins to be bestowed upon him; it could mean that the never-ending battle with envy is beginning again.

Recognition of Envy

To deal with envy in ourselves and others we have to be able to discern its appearances. Recognizing envy in others seems to present no problem. All of us recall occasions on which we met with envy. But how many incidences escaped our awareness? Perhaps we saw only the cruder manifestations; these were so blatant that we could not help but be aware of them. Or we may remember only situations in which we ourselves were the victims of envious behavior. Envy was painfully brought home to us then. Say someone cheated us out of a promotion by envious slander. A teacher gave us a bad grade because he was envious of our brightness, good looks, or family background. Examples like these can be multiplied. Feeling the pinch of envy, we find it less difficult to spot its source. But is envy always that recognizable? What about our own envy?

Again we may be well aware of crude manifestations of envy in ourselves. We may feel its pang when we realize that our neighbors can afford delightful cruises while we have to stay home or, at most, visit some dull relatives eighty miles away. But what about our more subtle envious leanings?

If anything, envy seems to be one of the tendencies we try most to conceal. The face of envy may hide behind masks of reasonableness and modesty, wisdom and common sense. To uncover envy in its innocent appearances is a must for anyone who wants to overcome envy in himself and others. When we say "overcoming envy in others," we do not mean, of course, that we can free them from the pain of envy. That is a question of each man's personal growth. We mean that a relaxed awareness of another's envy can help us not to arouse it unnecessarily. This calm awareness may enable us also to foresee the effects of envy once it comes into play. Such insight will help us to respond wisely to envy, to mitigate the impact of envious words or deeds.

Before we discuss some disguises of envy, we can ask ourselves why people want to deny this feeling. An obvious answer is that they are ashamed of it. It does not look nice to be envious. This answer may explain the need for concealment but it does not get to the root of the problem. Why are we ashamed? Because our friends and colleagues would look down on us if they would know how envious we were? But what about the envy hidden within us that we disguise from ourselves, that we do not own up to? Nobody would ever know about it. Why then is it covered up? Why did we begin to repress our awareness of these feelings in us at a certain moment of our life? Is there something in the feeling of envy itself that makes us afraid to admit to ourselves that we are envious?

Let's say I'm the administrator of a small business. I share its administration with a pleasant fellow as skillful as I but one who happens to be more faithful to his originality. Due to all kinds of experiences in childhood, I am suspicious of my own spontaneity. I come from a strait-laced family. My parents frowned upon any deed, thought, or feeling that seemed out of bounds. "Out of bounds" to them meant anything that did not correspond with their stereotyped principles of conduct. I could not easily be myself. As a result I am still wary of my own spontaneity. Such wariness interferes with the free and flexible use of my skills and talents. Like my parents, I am not so much self-motivated as moved by some sturdy provincial ways of the past, for no more reason than that they are of the past.

My companion is luckier. He is not obsessed by the family inhibitions that tie my hands, to say nothing about the restraints they put on my fantasies, thoughts, and feelings. He can be wholly in the moment. His involvement in the business at hand makes him astute, intuitive, and flexible in the split second decisions he has to make. He operates at the peak of his capacity. He is as zealous, skillful, and talented as I. We share these talents equally, but his originality and spontaneity have free play while mine are repressed. It is painful to experience daily his ease of life. I envy him.

"I envy him" means, among other things, that I feel that he is superior to me. If I allow myself to admire his loyalty to himself, I will be inclined to evaluate myself in light of this quality. The right thing for me would be to profess simply that in certain areas of life I am clearly less spontaneous than my companion. This is a difficult confession to make. Having been raised in a competitive society, it pains me to admit that certain aspects of life are not open to competition. Let us say that I would be able to bypass the inhibitions of my past. Even then my originality would still be different from his and from that of everyone else's.

Admitting my envy is admitting that somebody else is superior to me in some way. This is an act of humility. Humility is a rare commodity in a civilization built upon the pride of achievement by self-made men. Genuine humility is possible only in secure people. But security may be as scarce as humility.

Our competitive society instills a basic insecurity in people. Insecurity is one of the shaping forces of our civilization. To overcome insecurity people reach out for status, position, possession, education, so that they can feel that they have made it and that their children will make it in turn. They compete with each other for these symbols of achievement. They acquire such symbols by their contribution to the production of goods and services. The rewards and promotions they obtain in exchange make them feel more safe and certain of themselves.

To counteract feelings of uncertainty a person may become a voracious consumer. The more rewards he reaps from his contributions to the production process, the more he needs to show these rewards to others. He buys expensive houses, cars, clothes, food, trips, entertainment. Through them he cries out, as it were: "See what I can allow myself, how well I have made it, how well established I am!"

Insecurity keeps the processes of production and consumption in high gear. It is crucial for a consumer society that people maintain a basic insecurity that cannot be resolved by any increase in status or possession. Such increases are meant to assuage momentarily the insecurity that is eating away at the average person in our culture. The reaching of a certain status is not meant to remedy, nor should it remedy, the fundamental insecurity of Western man. Otherwise he might no longer feel compelled to augment his production and consumption in order to increase his rewards and recognition.

Insecurity cannot be taken away by enlarged remunerations. It is rooted in the non-awakening of man's originality as a human being. He does not know who he is. He does not know what he wants. He does not know what is best for him. He knows what he can become in the eyes of producers and consumers who comprise the anonymous public.

Admitting My Envy

Against this background it is easy to see why I cannot admit envy to myself. This admission would mean that I am in some ways inferior. As a basically insecure Western man, to admit inferiority in any respect is too much for me to take. Especially is this true in regard to envy of originality.

The original self of another person may be superior to my original self, at least in certain dimensions. To admit to myself that I am envious of originality would mean in this case to admit that I feel inferior. But my culture has suggested that we are all basically alike, that differences are due only to good luck, right timing, right education, right backing, cunning, or hard work. This explanation of differences is less offensive to my ego. It is surely less threatening to my already shaky feeling of self-esteem than to admit to an inferiority in regard to that human originality which manifests itself above and beyond skillful performance. According to this argument, in the last analysis nobody is better than I in anything. If I had the same luck, the same backing, I would be as well off as that other fellow or even better. It is all a question of skill and not of a uniqueness that may speak in and through this skill.

To recognize fully my envy of originality would mean to recognize that I am different and perhaps in some ways inferior to the envied person. I can admit this to the degree that I have found and accepted my own uniqueness, whether or not I can express it in a performance that is striking and impressive.

If I can work this envy of mine through, it can become respect. Envy of originality presupposes the discovery of the original value of another. If I feel no longer threatened or diminished by this value, I may come to respect it. Envy is potential respect. Respect, in turn, can initiate an enriching interaction between me and other valuable people loyal to their uniqueness. The opposite is true too: respect is potential envy. Respect is the acknowledgment of an original value in the other as value. At the moment that this acknowledgment begins to threaten me and to make me feel inferior, respect may turn into envy.

Envy of originality is thus related to the way I feel about myself. My self-esteem is at stake. I want to assert myself because somehow the original presence of the other has shaken my feeling of worth.

When a person lives his true originality, his life becomes a striking expression of humble self-assertion. To be one's best self is an effortless assertion of what one is called to be. This self-assertion is permeated in turn by the humble awareness that I often fail my calling and may never live up to it perfectly. This self-assertion becomes for me a natural, unassuming experience. It is difficult for others to doubt such a fine testimony of selfhood.

Childhood and Envy

One reason why many of us do not live on a relaxed level of self-acceptance can be traced to childhood. As children, we develop—over and above our given originality—a quasi originality. School, family, and neighborhood make us feel, think, and behave in certain ways. Such ways may be at odds with who we truly are. Nevertheless they are deeply inculcated in us. We may end up with a set of thoughts, sentiments, and attitudes opposed to our original gifts. They are invested with such a motivating force that we may feel compelled to live totally out of this structure of alien motivations. This sediment of borrowed motivations covers up our spontaneous tendencies. It may prove fatal for the growth of our personality, for the spontaneity we have repressed as children is the prefiguration of our possible self-motivations.

Instead of our own spontaneity, this secondary layer becomes the breeding ground, the learned origin, of our thoughts and actions. Our true self remains hidden. For it we substitute an imposed or quasi originality. This quasi originality is reinforced and expanded by later choices we make in the course of our lives.

The quasi originality of childhood is for a great part determined by the prejudices of the society into which I am born and which have shaped the behavior of my parents and of other people in my neighborhood. My later choices are deeply affected by the same society because its influence ties in with the quasi originality I developed already as a child.

Ego-Affirmation and Ego-Envy

Because quasi originality cannot be truly mine, it is shot through with uncertainty. I am not sure of myself on the deepest level of my life. I fight that uncertainty by asserting myself on the ego level. The ego represents my practical and conceptual achievements within the culture. Every time I accomplish something that can be acknowledged by my society, I experience a feeling of ego-affirmation. Because I am so unsure about the real me, I need such ego-affirmations badly. They may be the only thing I have.

I meet people caught in the same predicament. Like me, they substituted early in life a quasi originality for their true uniqueness. They are as basically insecure as I am. Like me, their sense of worth depends on ego-affirmations.

When I meet one of my own kind at a dinner party, for example, we start our conversation with a pleasant exchange of ego-affirmations. We tell each other about the marvelous things we have been doing or about the house, car, or vacation we can afford, the important people with whom we associate. The latter exercise of extolling one's ego-affirmative contacts is called "name-dropping." The other party shows polite admiration for these ego-affirmations and, in so doing, adds to the over-all affirmation I need to feel secure. Then he in turn tells me, modestly, of course, about his own feats. If we play the game of mutual affirmation well, we embellish each other's tales with admiring interjections.

After this ceremony of mutual affirmation, we may go on to the phase of joint ego-affirmation. Now we extol the excellence of the views we share and the things we have in common. We exalt others who happen to share the same kind of achievement. During our conversation, we condemn, ridicule, or suavely belittle those who have not reached this height or whose approaches are at odds with the style in which we seek our security.

The continuous process of individual and mutual ego-affirmation that takes place in our society is, of course, veiled. We cover it up with all kinds of secondary motivations, such as telling the truth, getting to know each other, serving charitable and religious enterprises, unmasking the enemies of the common good.

No amount of ego-affirmation can take away our basic insecurity. What is missing is a spontaneous self-assertion which coincides with simply being myself. As long as I meet people like me, who put their whole trust and worth in ego-affirmations and who continue to confirm me in the same way, I may live on in an aura of make-believe security and quasi self-esteem.

The scene shifts drastically when I meet a person who has the poise of true self-assertion, who is little impressed by the ego-affirmations I and my friends are so enamored of.

Many fairy tales, novels, and legends have portrayed this aspect of life. Remember Cinderella. All she owned was her simple self. Her stepmother and stepsisters were proud of the ego-affirmative things they possessed: their house and clothes, their standing in the neighborhood. The prince, however, and life itself, as symbolized by the fairy godmother, fell in love with Cinderella because she was herself; she was true to life.

How deeply I may be affected when the simple originality of a person reminds me of the real me that I lost or never allowed to be. My ego-affirmations may not convince him about my worth as a person. He may appreciate them to a degree, but I sense that he looks beyond them to the real me. His personality makes me doubt myself. I may feel empty and frustrated. I may even feel furious with him.

His spontaneous self-assertion evokes in me the need for renewed ego-affirmations. I cannot bear to compare myself

with him on the self level. I want to bring the battle back to
the ego level. My envy of his selfhood now becomes dis-
placed by envy of the measurable things he has reached in
his life, partly as a result of his loyalty to himself. I deny this
deepest ground. I prefer to disregard his uniqueness and to
focus instead on his performance in isolation from the personal originality his performance happens to embody and
reveal. Now I am able to tell myself and others that I too
could have achieved these things if only his background,
his education, his good looks would have been mine.

In this way, by turning self-envy into ego-envy, I take
away the sting of envy of originality. I reduce the original
person to my unoriginal level. I can deal with him there. I
silence the summons to find myself. Instead I resort to more
and more strained ego-affirmations in the face of the other's
spontaneous self-assertion.

We should become aware of our tendency to turn self-
envy into ego-envy. The telltale symptom is that we begin to
assume that if only we had the same looks, position, salary,
the same family or education, we would have developed as
an original human being just as well as he. We may discover,
however, that our irritation with him remains, even if we
obtain all these things. Indeed, one of the ways to come to
genuine self-insight is to imagine what would happen if we
would acquire the ego-affirmative assets we pretend to envy.
Would we then really feel like mature, self-motivated men?
Would we no longer be irritated by the other's uniqueness
as a person?

Such a consideration may help us to admit the real object
of our envy, namely, the simple fact that this person is loyal
to his self-motivations and we are not. He is willing to sacrifice for the sake of this originality any ego-affirmations that
clash with it and we are not. We may grow to the insight
that we can never have his originality, that we should strive
to imitate not so much his originality as his search for uniqueness, his acceptance of selfhood, his loyalty to what he is.

We should not envy these characteristics but emulate them. Then we may find our own uniqueness; we may grow in faithfulness to our own deepest self, no matter what ego-affirmations we have to forgo in light of this loyalty.

In regard to the kind of ego performances in which we are called to express our newly discovered self, we should manifest a genuine but secondary interest—neither neglecting this choice nor making it an overriding concern. When our striving after ego-affirmation becomes intense, we may suspect that it is spurred on by envy. This envy may be about the ego-affirmations of somebody else; it may also emerge when a unique person appears on the horizon of our existence.

When we meet a man who lives in relaxed self-surrender, we may suddenly realize that genuine self-surrender is the same as spontaneous self-assertion on the deepest level of one's life. A person's uniqueness is a treasure of possibilities and an outline of limitations. To surrender to one's uniqueness as possibility and limitation is to live in inspiration and resignation, in active and passive strength.

Envy Within the Family Situation

Certain patterns of envy can be traced to their beginnings in childhood. When we speak about envy in childhood, we should be aware that it is not of the same nature as envy in the older child and in the adult. In them, envy is more deeply rooted. From what we have said about self-assertion, ego-affirmation, and the feeling of inferiority, it is clear that envy presupposes that the envious person has acquired a perception of himself that enables him to distinguish himself from others and, therefore, to compare himself with others, favorably or unfavorably. A person without any perception of himself as distinguished from others could never be envious because he could not compare himself with others. The more perception of self, as separated from others, is developed, deepened, and differentiated, the more the attitude of envy can become a possibility in the life of the person. Children do not as yet have a well-differentiated self-perception. Envy in them cannot be a deeply rooted personal attitude. In children, we can only speak of situations, periods, or incidences of envy. If these are prolonged, they may spell the beginning of lasting patterns. With this reservation in mind, let us look again at envy in childhood.

The child has many opportunities for envy. They correspond with the countless occasions he finds for respect, the counterpole of envy. To be a child is to be small and dependent. Childhood is a time of learning from people who are far more powerful than the child himself. They seem able to do almost anything they want. They are a source of food and life, of shelter and clothing. The child cannot grasp the inner meaning of originality as lived by his parents. He has only a vague, almost mythical apprehension that they are in some way the powerful origin of his daily life. He may sense similarly, in a concrete bodily way, that his older brothers and sisters can originate changes in their own and in his situation—changes that he cannot originate himself. It is clear from many observations that the child can be envious of his parents or of his brothers and sisters in a child-like fashion.

What happens in the child when he responds to the superiority of others in the family with envy? An envious response is negative. It is a confession to oneself that one is less than others and that one can really do nothing about it. This belief may keep a child inert. He may abandon any attempt to grow in the direction of the maturity attained by others. Why should he risk effort or growth? Envy precludes emulation of the envied person. The child stops growing, as it were. Instead, he demands the same equal attention, praise and reward, rights and privileges, as others without doing anything to deserve this or without patiently waiting for the process of growth.

The child cannot yet know the necessity of such things

as waiting patiently for growth. It is for this reason that envy in childhood is such a normal occurrence. One cannot wholly avoid its emergence. All one can guard against is an unnecessary arousal or continuation of envy.

Once envy is evoked, we should do all in our power to prevent its prolongation. When the child is kept in a continuous state of envy, it can become a lifelong affliction.

Sustained envy in childhood hinders the child's unfolding. It interferes with the two main conditions for his growth. First of all, there should be respect between the child and his parents. Respect in this case does not have the same meaning it has for the older child and the adult. Respect in the young child means that he does not envy the superiority of his parents, that is to say, he gives up the aggressive striving to acquire at once all that his parents are and possess. Respect in childhood means that the child goes along with the fact that his parents are more powerful than he, that they are somehow the sustaining origin of his daily life and growth. Childlike respect signifies a spontaneous compliance with his parents' attempts to teach him. There is a readiness on his part to emulate the standards they set for him in regard to learning how to eat, crawl, talk, how to walk and dress himself. All of the above is included in the term "childlike respect," which is the pristine form or prefiguration of respect in later life. As we already know, respect is the opposite of envy; both envy and respect are directed toward the same end, namely, toward that which is experienced as uniquely superior in the other and valuable in itself. Childlike respect is a first condition for true growth in the child. If this attitude toward parental superiority is replaced by its opposite, envy, growth cannot take place.

The second condition for the growth of the child is that of spontaneous appropriation, an ability which depends on the respectful attitude toward superiority we have just spoken about. When respect, even childlike respect, is genuine and spontaneous, it leads to a natural participation in

the respected superior value witnessed in the other. Respect
is an attitude of looking and looking again in appreciation,
of trying to participate in values that are experienced as good.
Clearly respect implies a natural movement toward personal
appropriation of the appreciated value insofar as this is
possible.

For the young child, this respectful emulation is only true
in an analogical sense. In him, the movement of respect and
appropriation is without self-awareness and freedom, without inner struggle and planning. It is not really a personal
movement; it is rather a pre-personal spontaneous orientation toward value that can be fostered or hampered by his
parents or by those who take their place. Only later in life
can this pre-personal orientation favorable for growth become a personal, free attitude. It is clear, however, that a
child in whom this pre-personal respectful and appropriative
attitude was fostered is more likely to affirm this attitude
personally for the remainder of his life.

True learning is possible only on the basis of personal
appropriation of the things to be learned. Personal appropriation is difficult, if not impossible, in the absence of respect for the person to be imitated or to be taught by. It
surely becomes impossible when respect is not only absent
but replaced by its radical opposite, envy. Envy cuts the
child off from the envied one, in this case his father or
mother. As a result, it inhibits both respect and spontaneous
appropriation of the valuable skills and attitudes the parents
have to teach him. The child that grows older may still be
possessed by envy in regard to his parents. The older child
may then refuse to appropriate tentatively some of the self-
motivations of his parents as possible motivations for himself. The development of self-motivation—first by selective
and tentative imitation—is essential for the discovery and unfolding of a person's uniqueness. Envy would make such
appropriation impossible.

Out of envy a child may give up his attempts to learn a

certain skill. There are cases of children whose talking, walking, or dressing are delayed because they are obsessed by envy. The same is true later in life. Some students cannot really learn or even hear what a teacher has to say. In certain cases this deafness may be due to envy. Instead of trying to participate in his wisdom to the degree of their possibilities, they resort to an ostentatious display of ego-affirmation.

The child who refuses to learn because of envy finds himself in a vicious circle, especially when his envy extends from his parents to his brothers and sisters and to others in his surroundings. One must learn also from others. No one can be his own exclusive source of growth. The child who envies others, the child who estranges himself from those more highly developed than he, may alienate himself from all sources of growth.

Envy compels him to give up learning; he lags behind others who keep on growing. But the beginning of envy was precisely his frustrating awareness of their superiority. Now that he refuses to learn because of his envy, the distance between his inferiority and their superiority becomes greater and greater. As a result he becomes more and more envious. Increased envy in turn makes it increasingly difficult for him to learn. And wholehearted learning, personal appropriation, would be the path to his deliverance.

Dynamics of Childhood Envy in Relation to Adult Life

By reflecting on patterns of childhood envy, we obtain light about envy in adult life. The dynamics of envy in childhood can reappear. They may stultify a man's growth.

I remember a student who could have become an outstanding psychologist were it not for envy. Envy made it impossible for him to learn anything from anyone superior to him. Like many students, he was eager to become an original man. But John's desire was not to find his deepest self in dialogue with values that were already lived by others more accomplished than he. His desire for originality was an ego project. He wanted to look original, to be conspicuous as an inventive person, to be called creative by fellow students and colleagues. He was impatiently grasping for a status which could become his only after long reflection and intense study under advanced teachers. When John had to face a truly creative teacher, he could not admit to himself that this man was original. He envied him. But he could not admit his envy to himself.

Admitting feelings of envy would amount to confessing at least to himself, "I feel inferior to that person. I hate his superiority. I cannot stand his originality because it reminds me painfully that I am not yet that original and that perhaps I may never be able to compete with that kind of man. Admitting his superiority exposes me to the admittance that there may be many others who like him are superior to me. I cannot bear the threat that there may be a whole group of people whose originality I can never emulate. There is only one way open to me to escape this threat and my frustration. I must deny his superiority. I must tell myself that somehow I am better. I must destroy his reputation at least in my own mind by associating with other famous psychologists elsewhere. I will praise them to level him."

And so it goes with John. Of course, he would never say or think such things consciously. Here speaks his unconscious train of thought as suggested by his equally unconscious envy. His envy made it impossible for him to really learn from his gifted teacher. He could have learned considerably by loyal and respectful participation in the living thought of this obliging man. He was a professor always willing to spend part of his class time to answer questions. He could have obtained first-hand explanations of his teacher's way of thought, experience, perception. Instead he neglected all these possibilities in favor of dabbling in some more famous but long dead author. Or he spent his days in exclusive preoccupation with notable authors still alive but far away and not available for consultation. Even the papers John wrote were written in spite. He was always trying to trip up his mentor by defending opposite theories of others whom he only half understood.

In the course of his study, John learned almost nothing. The tragedy was that this process of envious comparison repeated itself over and over again in his life. Every time he met a teacher, supervisor, or colleague superior to him and a possible source of growth, he would fall into the same predicament. He would spend all his time spiting this person by comparing him in an invidious way to other men of fame.

I have not seen John for a long time, but I would not be surprised if he still lives in envious comparison, still unable to grow in spite of talents. John's pattern of envy may go back to a childhood situation. One wonders if perhaps psychotherapy may someday liberate him from the vicious circle in which he is caught.

Dealing with Childhood Envy

As soon as we become aware that a child of ours is obsessed by envy, we should ponder how to create a family situation in which the child is less overwhelmed by the superiority of others. A parent can be ostentatious about his superiority. A child feels threatened by the power of his parents when this power is accompanied by self-preoccupation and indifference toward himself. The parents seem unapproachable. Diminished is the natural flow of trust and respect a child can feel toward them. Instead the child feels lost, unwanted. He may react to this feeling with envy of what they have and what they seem to withhold from him. Envy then blocks the natural movement of respectful surrender to the values represented by his parents.

Sometimes the child's growth in envy is due to estrangement between the parents themselves. Mother and father may be so preoccupied with their own conflicts and frustrations that they are less and less available to him. They become for him figures of a faraway superiority that withholds itself in a strange and tense world of its own. It is usually not sufficient for the parents to pretend that there is no conflict at all. Children sense the tension that is in the air. In many cases one of the parents may still be able to relate well enough to the child to prevent the emergence of a prolonged and stubborn envy. In other cases the only solution may be for the parents to seek professional help to solve their problems and hopefully ease the growing stubbornness of their child.

If I am faced with a similar case of stubborn envy in a student, acquaintance, colleague, or employee, I may not be able to do much about it. Being aware of the dynamics of such situations may lessen somewhat the painful impact of envious disparagement I have to suffer from these people. The same insight may help me to treat their envious tactics with a casualness that makes them less inclined to continue them. If an occasion arises when I can sit down with such a person and make him see what is bothering him, that would be splendid. But such an opportunity may not present itself. Untimely attempts on that score are likely to be met with scorn.

Lastly, what can I do when I become aware that I myself suffer from this envious disposition? A promise of improvement is precisely the fact that I begin to suspect this affliction in myself. This pattern of envy is usually an unconscious process. Hence to bring it to awareness is a step in the right direction.

Reading this book, as we've suggested, may give some people an inkling of their own envy. Seeing the dynamics of envy magnified in unusual cases, one may become aware of the minute and subtle signs of the same dynamics in his own life. Once I spot these manifestations I should from time to time reflect on them. I can dwell on the dynamics of envy and try in a relaxed way to find out in what measure they apply to me even in minor ways. Reading and reflection may make me sensitive to the emergence of envy in my everyday life. In the beginning I may discover a few unrelated events. Slowly the evidence will mount. After a period of patient observation, I may see emerge an envious pattern. I may begin to see how this pattern has stunted my growth and happiness, my spontaneity and peace of mind. I may be motivated to work this pattern through, gradually liberating myself from it. The daily attempt to achieve self-liberation will help me gain new insights into my personality. These too will enable me to grow beyond the prison of envious self-isolation. Helpful as a sounding board may be a wise and compassionate friend.

As always, certain cases of deeply rooted envy may be relieved only by therapy or counseling. Certain types of group therapy and group dynamics, under professional supervision, may be enlightening. Members of the group may point out to me how isolated and uncommunicative I am when I demonstrate unwittingly a sample of my envious behavior in the group.

Children Envied by Parents

We must also say a few words about the case in which the roles are reversed. That is, instead of the child envying his parents, the parents envy their child. Envy here works like a chain reaction. The links of the chain are the successive generations of the family plagued by envy. One generation exemplifies the life style of envy for the next one. If the next generation does not find a solution for this problem, it may continue the same life style and impose it upon the next generation in turn. How does this transference come about?

It is certainly not true that a child inherits envy. Neither does he learn directly the inner envious response to people who appear superior to him. He may learn directly how to speak disparagingly about people who are seen as superior by his parents. But that does not mean that he learns directly the attitude of envy itself with its peculiar sentiments and perceptions.

Parents possessed by an envious attitude that orients their entire life can direct this attitude toward the child. Anything that naturally evokes respect will arouse its opposite, envy, in the person who refuses to honor superiority. When the child shows a superior quality his parents have belittled in others, they are only too ready to belittle it in him.

I remember a man whose brothers and sisters went through college successfully. Afterwards they did well in various fields. He himself was less brilliant during his high school years. He was a mediocre student, but still he could have made college if he had tried a little harder. A college degree would have been for him the key to a moderately successful life in the professional world. However, he was so envious of the brilliance of his brothers and sisters that he felt compelled to deny the value of education, the very usefulness of learning. To spite them and the whole hated world of educated people, he left high school in anger. He refused to prepare himself for anything other than a low-paying menial job. He married a woman obsessed by the same envious preoccupation. They had a child who showed a natural brightness, a spontaneous interest in learning. Not so surprisingly, he aroused the envious attitude of his parents. They debunked his attempts to better himself educationally. They spoke disparagingly of his well-educated aunts and uncles. Their reaction bewildered the child. It interfered with his self-discovery. To believe and follow his parents meant for him to falsify his own interest in learning, to forgo the desires that spontaneously emerged in him. He submitted to the view of his parents. He began to imitate their ego-affirmative gestures. It was not long before their envious attitude became his.

To be sure, this development could have been different.

He could have found other people to follow, such as one of his disparaged uncles or aunts. But to expect such an independent choice on the part of a vulnerable child may be asking too much. One way to help a person who is the victim of such a distortion in childhood is to present him with opportunities to rediscover his own tendencies before these are veiled by the envious life orientation of his parents.

The Obviously Original Child in a Leveling Society

A child may be so original that no amount of leveling in the family can erase his spontaneity. His uniqueness shows itself, moreover, in unusual interests, behavior, and performance. As a result, the child evokes envy inside and outside the family. Once he becomes an early object of envy, he is prone to all kinds of disturbances in his development which we must now consider.

Children in a leveling society are raised to adjust themselves indiscriminately to that society. No doubt children or adolescents may rebel as a group against adults. The leveling society allows for some standard rebellion of all the average young against the old. The subculture that is allowed to rebel nevertheless shows in its structure the same features as the homogenizing society as a whole. Children may be defiant as a group, but woe to the gifted child or adolescent who dares to be himself in an original way within the group.

Let's say the rebellious group likes rock music. The moment a member of the gang dares to let on that he likes classical music, he exposes himself to being branded a "square." The gang likes noisy togetherness at every moment of the day; he sometimes prefers solitude. He enjoys books his fellows do not like and so stands silently condemned. When his conversation shows an unusual view of people and things, they feel he is not "with it." They look at him and snicker. He feels apart from the others. He may not be insensitive to their interests. He might even want to be like them but he cannot. It is not a matter of feeling that he is better or worse than they but of knowing he is different. He may be as aware of everyday values as others but cannot live their immediacy as intensely and exclusively.

The regular kids seem secure and at ease. They seem lucky kids, easily accepted by peers and parents, liked by teachers, clergymen, and other representatives of the normal leveling society. They are not considered "oddballs" like him. They never seem disturbed by original thoughts, feelings, and fantasies. Yet, strangely, they are considered the interesting kids while he strikes others as a dud. This aspect of his reputation may always remain a mystery to him. How can others find these kids interesting when, from his limited exceptional viewpoint, he finds them so boring.

Many disturbances may occur when a child discovers his reputation as an obviously original fellow in a leveling society. This discovery sets him apart from the common run of children or teen-agers in his circle. Such disturbances are not due to his originality as such. Other children may be original and self-motivated too. What makes his originality obvious—and often irritating—are the rather exceptional interests, sensitivities, and talents through which his originality shows itself. Some of his problems may be the outcome of the way in which people look at such unusual expressions.

It is difficult for a child to handle a bad reputation, a reputation of which he is not guilty and about which he can do nothing. He may meet an understanding parent, teacher, or friend who will kindly encourage him and tell him to be grateful for his gifts—in the meantime helping him toward adaptation. His mentor may show delight that he is a child with an innocent eye, an eye not perverted in its spontaneous seeing by the stereotypes of a pragmatic society. Now the child does not know who to believe. He is torn between joy and sadness. With many people he feels like an outcast. But the rare understanding person makes him feel that he is "in" with humanity on a deeper level. One thing is sure, no matter what he says or does, his reputation follows him.

If, as a result of his isolation, disturbances do develop, some people may ascribe them to the unusual expressions of his originality. "You could expect that to happen to such an oddball," they will say. "He would be all right if he would play like the other kids. He should keep his nose out of the books." They are really saying he should be a perfect copy of all the nice kids in the neighborhood raised by nice parents in a nice community. They seem to forget that this child did not ask for such spontaneous, precocious, one-sided expressions of his uniqueness. Compassion instead of derision would perhaps have prevented his disturbances.

The educator or school psychologist may unfortunately complete the misunderstanding begun at home. His profession gives him the aura of authority. Nonetheless, he may be only a well-paid representative of the functional society who believes that perfect adjustment, or leveling out the last trace of uniqueness, is the highest wisdom. What can the child in its helplessness do against such an array of powers? For some exceptional children, the only way out may be a flight from the leveling process into mental illness. There in the hospital, they find a carefully isolated place where one is allowed or even supposed to be different.

The child whose expressions of originality are exceptional will also meet envy. Envy makes people cruel toward him. The suspicion that he is or feels himself in certain ways superior to them may upset other children and adults. His unusual self-experience and expression may challenge their own feelings of superiority over him in functional interaction, practical adjustment, regular fellowship, sports and academic performance, should they happen to be better than he in these areas.

The unusual child is thus early in life faced with the ambiguous attitudes of others toward his exceptional expressions of originality. He is perplexed and not yet able to invent modes of adaptation that could prevent these jolting reactions. Flexible adaptation could help him to develop a life style faithful to his originality and its peculiar expression, while assuring him some acceptance by others. Such an adaptive life style would prevent in him the poisonous spread of bitterness toward those who envy him. A child is too young, too inexperienced to take this kind of stand. He may lose tenderness, develop defensiveness, pride, paranoia—attitudes which isolate him more than necessary from his companions.

Later on he will be faced with a twofold task. First he must reflect on the envious life situation in a mature way. He must find out how he can live with the least detriment to himself and others. Secondly, he must consider the ineffective attitudes which he developed in childhood toward envious people. He must ask himself: "What is my life style now as a result of my childhood experiences and of my reactions to them? How can I change my life in such a way that I will be less in conflict with others?"

The Role of Envy in the Social Development of the Child

Normal incidents of envy happen regularly between children that are not too different from one another in self-expression. This kind of envy is universal; it plays a definite role in the social development of child and society.

Childhood envy of originality can help the child to learn social skills. Envy is a negative attitude. As such, it does not teach the child compassion with the pain of envy he evokes in others. Neither can envy as such help the envied child to come to inner harmony and relaxed self-discipline. Nonetheless, childhood envy can make some indirect contribution to his socialization. True social behavior is rooted in a mature motivation to care for others out of wisdom and love. However, the implementation of this social motivation in daily life demands social skills. Such skills are neutral by themselves. They can be used for the implementation of social as well as anti-social motivations.

A good example of one such social skill is the art of diplomacy. I can be diplomatic in a genuine attempt to foster relaxed relations with others. Such relations sustain better social living. Diplomacy can just as well be abused for selfish purposes. The diplomatic person may use his skill only to enhance himself at the cost of others.

A person may initially develop a social skill like diplomacy for selfish motives. He may later use the same skill in the service of positive social motivation. In the case of childhood envy of originality, we find a striking example. One of the skills necessary for social behavior is that of self-control. A truly social man controls himself. He avoids words or deeds that would unnecessarily arouse envy in others. It pains him to pain others. He has developed a personal kind of self-discipline in regard to original expressions that may irritate people unnecessarily.

Not only the individual person but also society as a whole promotes social behavior. Society tries to control unjust attempts to use one's expressions of originality to become rich and powerful at the expense of the rest of society. This is a social type of control. Its enforcement is demanded by the majority. Such control concerns itself with the emergence of irresponsible individualism that would threaten social peace, justice, and good fellowship. Both kinds of control—personal and social—may begin to develop in childhood when children deal with the appearance of original behavior in their midst.

Children envious of the attractive manifestations of spontaneity in some of their peers try to keep these utterances within bounds by demanding equality. This demand is one factor leading to the acceptance of a certain control of individualism in society. The children whose envy is evoked by others devise among themselves social controls such as ridicule, disapproval, and rejection. Such controls mitigate the others' expression of their originality. They become more cautious in the use of their spontaneity to obtain favors from adults who are touched by their "cuteness."

Social controls are neutral. They can be used or abused; they can foster true or false social life. Social life can deteriorate into a cover for envy. Then social life abuses social controls; it represses the originality of others unnecessarily. It condemns self-motivation even when modestly manifested.

Childhood envy can also lead to the development of inner personal controls in the envied child himself. The child soon learns to avoid the envy of his brothers and playmates, for their resentment isolates him. He tries to moderate the expression of his originality. In this way he acquires some self-control. Again this skill is neutral. The self-discipline acquired in childhood can be abused by the original person as a trick to deceive people around him. It becomes an anti-social attitude. On the other hand, while growing up, the original child may become motivated by true compassion for those less in tune with their originality than he or less able to express it through special talents of performance and communication. He tries to avoid hurting them by tempering words and actions that are sure to arouse envy in them unnecessarily. In this case, his skill of self-control becomes a truly personal and social attitude, arising out of his care for others.

Originally he may have developed self-control out of anxiety. As long as anxiety about the envy and aggression of others remains the only source of self-discipline, such discipline will remain a repressive force in the child's personality. Its effect will be negative. Nevertheless, such self-control—even when wrongly motivated—will promote skills of self-discipline which may become more positive in content later on. Healthy development is characterized by a transition from control of the expression of originality out of anxiety to control out of respect for oneself and others.

The mature person knows that no man can be himself without evoking some envy in others. The self-motivated man learns not to evoke envy unnecessarily. He also knows how to bear with the envy that is unavoidable if he is to be true to himself. The first art implies the strength of modesty, the second that of fortitude.

Mitigation of Envy and the Expression of Originality

Up to this moment we have indicated the various patterns of envy and of being envied which may develop in a man's life. We have also mentioned possible ways of ameliorating the painful situations that are the consequence of envy. As we know, however, certain people will always have to bear with the pain of envy. Loyalty to their own originality, especially when its spontaneous expression is exceptional, will not allow them to escape this suffering lastingly. The only thing they can hope for is to mitigate envy. They must become aware of their reputation as exceptionally original men, which—in our kind of society—may mean the same thing as having a bad reputation.

Still the original man must learn to live with his originality graciously; he must learn how to diminish the bad effects of this reputation on himself and on those dear to him. He must be especially aware that his predicament makes him vulnerable as a person. If he is not careful, he may distort his life because of unnecessary anger, aggressiveness, or defensiveness in response to the bad reputation imputed to him.

The envied man must not merely survive in society. He must develop into an harmonious person. Harmony is a precarious balance of counterpoints. To be oneself in an envious society inevitably means that one must live a life of contrasts—of solitude and sharing, of compassion and courage, of caution and spontaneity. A person faithful to himself must seek solitude without isolation, communion without loss of selfhood. He must not fear the blows of envy, yet must shy away from words and deeds which evoke it unnecessarily. Not unduly preoccupied with his own reputation, he must remain concerned with the reputation of his family, friends, employees, or students—all those whose fate is linked with his. What envy does to him, it does to them. They may not be ready, as he is, to bear with envious detraction. For their sake, he must often be satisfied with a hidden life among his peers, a life of discretion, silent about his personal experiences and creative enterprises. But constant discretion must not detract from effective performance, from his spontaneity and ease of mind.

This may seem an impossible program; nevertheless the difficulty of living as an original person in the present age must be faced. Many never make it. Some succumb to the collectivity. Others become embittered. Still others withdraw in a futile attempt to be faithful to themselves in isolation.

How can I live my selfhood in harmony with the demands of my original commitment? Much is dependent on my life situation and the way I respond to it. My attitudes develop in response to people, events, and things as they appear in my life. I can adapt my style of original living to my surroundings, at least to some degree. Before applying this principle to the living of my uniqueness, let us illustrate it by an example of how I can live another quality—for example, my generosity. How I should express my generosity depends partly on my life situation. It depends also on my inner stance, on the make-up of my personality.

If I am emotional, outgoing, and talkative, my giving takes on warmth, feeling, and spontaneity compared to the giving of a man who by temperament is more rational, reserved, and to the point. The style of my generosity is also affected by my culture and environment. The way in which a native of Italy gives himself to others is different from the style in which a fourth-generation Italian living in New England expresses his generosity. Why the difference?

Giving does not occur in a vacuum. An exuberant manifestation of giving in Boston may be met with raised eyebrows. People may joke about it. So I try to be sensitive to their feelings. To prevent this from happening a second time, I temper the manner of my giving. The way I express my generosity thus has a history. It changes because of my attempts to adapt to the ways of others. It takes into account their reactions. It responds accordingly. This development is by no means automatic.

A girl wants to live her generosity out in social action. She volunteers for work in South America. She gives without sparing herself. In spite of this, people do not like her. They find her stand-offish, cool, a "typical Yankee." She feels hurt. After all, she did not come so far for the fun of it. She came to help these people. At home in New Hampshire, they had even ridiculed her for her exaggerated generosity. Gradually it dawns on her that she can only live effectively among these people if she tries to put some warmth into her social activities. After some time she is able to do so. She overcomes the antipathy of this outgoing population. Of course, she cannot match their exuberance. This would be unnatural for her. They don't expect that from her. Interestingly enough, the new warmth she feels spills over into the rest of her behavior. To her surprise, when she returns to the United States, her folks and friends comment on how she has changed, how different her personality is from when she left them. This is an example of how the expression of one's personality in one dimension can affect his personality as a whole.

Let us now apply the same principle to the adaptive living of one's originality.

I may have to live as an original person in a functional civilization. My skill in self-expression makes my originality obvious. My life style ought then to be influenced by the way in which average men in this society look upon a unique person in their midst. As a self-motivated man, able to express his originality spontaneously and obviously, I may be vigorously attacked and feebly defended. I begin to sense early in life that I am a threat to the collectivity; it wants to destroy the unusual person. My originality carries with it a kind of bad reputation, imposed on me from the first moment that people begin to discover that I am not a regular guy but a person who is rather unique. I cannot free myself from the stigma of this reputation no matter what I do.

A reputation in this sense is a vague composite of traits which a certain group of people ascribe to those outside their group. These traits are not necessarily real. They may be the product of the envy, anger, anxiety, and defensiveness of the group.

Certain white men may ascribe a whole collection of unfavorable traits to blacks which together make up their public image. As soon as a white citizen of this community finds out that a new neighbor is black, he may automatically impute to him this standard reputation. The black man cannot escape this image. He may build up all kinds of secondary reputations. He may be known for his honesty and his zeal, his fine family life, his skill as a businessman, or his academic excellence. Nevertheless, he always keeps the basic reputation of being a black man in a white community with whatever unfavorable traits this may carry in the minds of prejudiced people.

As an exceptionally expressive, self-motivated man in a leveling community, I may find myself in a similar predicament. I may be isolated unwittingly from others. Every self-motivated man will experience being isolated by envious people. This isolation was and still is more strikingly true for extraordinarily original men of all ages. One need only study the lives of Da Vinci, Mozart, Hammarskjöld, Kierkegaard, and others to witness this. While they may have enjoyed public and professional esteem, they went through long periods of deprecation by average classmates, colleagues, neighbors, and family members who considered them conceited, bizarre, or slightly mad. Their experience illustrates in large what can happen to a less original man on a smaller scale. People impose on him a reputation which he does not recognize himself, a reputation which is alien to him and which alienates him from others.

An obviously original man can react to the hostile consciousness of the leveling society in many ways. He may associate only with other original men. Much to his detriment, he creates with them an exclusive community within the community. Such an association affirms the suspicion of average "regular fellows." It alienates the original man more than necessary. He becomes the "strange bird" that others predicted he would be. His creative associates are in the same predicament. The tight exclusive association they form together has the semblance of unity. In reality they are forced together. Their association is not natural. What they have in common is neither their past, their talents, their interests, nor their current occupations. All they share is the situation of being exceptionally original men in an unoriginal society. Theirs is often a defensive togetherness forced upon them by the constant suspicion of the public. The temptation to respond in this way is difficult to resist. Such original men share the fate of having to live in a community which treats them as oddballs. But, if they are not careful, in their shared isolation they may develop ways of life which are more odd than necessary.

Dilemma of the Original Man in Days to Come

The disguised suspicion original men may be faced with is not merely the incidental irritation of a few disgruntled people. The public as public finds it difficult to tolerate them. They don't fit. Deprecation of originality is thus always latent in a leveling society. It emerges together with the tendency to streamline the culture for consumption and production.

The person who meets such public displeasure may hope
that history will change this mentality. And indeed the development of technology and automation may create conditions more favorable for personal living. Automation may
relieve many people from the drudgery of repetitive chores.
People may only be necessary for key positions in which
they have to make personal decisions supportive of human
values—humane evaluations that cannot be made by the
automated machinery of tomorrow. Add to this the freeing
of man for more leisure time and we realize that there is
much hope for a self-motivated life in the future and for
perhaps a lessening of envy toward those who live their own
life.

Something similar can be said about the continuing refinement of technique and automation. Such refinement may
make it possible to vary indefinitely the character and design
of products to be offered to the consumer. It is even not unthinkable that the consumer may suggest the kind of thing
he personally wants; it may not be too costly for the differentiated machines of tomorrow to fulfill his wish. Such a
development of science, technique, and automation could
grant many more possibilities for the expression of one's
original choice and taste.

While all this may be true, the original man today is still
faced with his dilemma. Neither is it so sure that self-
motivated men will have no dilemma the moment technology creates superb conditions for personal living. In spite
of such conditions, people could refuse to live their own
lives. They may still want to do blindly what most other people are doing simply because most other people are doing it.
Those who deviate from an inane commonality may be even
more disliked in an automated society, which gives everyone
abundant room to be himself.

The dynamics of envy of originality are such that a man's
faithfulness to his best self arouses guilt feelings in those who
have forsaken their own potentiality for self-motivation.

When these impersonal people see a person who is loyal to himself, they may be painfully reminded of what they have lost. To silence the irritating voice of self-reproach, they lash out at him. Their envy becomes aggressive.

Especially when a society gives a person abundantly the material possibilities he needs to be himself is he less able to excuse himself for abandoning the direction of his life to an anonymous public. It is thus more difficult to repress the awareness of such abandonment of self in a society where advanced technology liberates man from the material need to level himself. In such a society, man will necessarily be more aware of his possibilities for originality. One of the prices he will have to pay for this awareness is an increase in the experience of self-reproach when he does not live up to his expanded potential. This in turn will necessitate a stronger repression of the inner reproach. To maintain this repression he will have to lash out more angrily at those who are true to themselves and remind him of the life he has missed. The fate of some collegial communes or communities today may be a forewarning of things to come. The collegial community may be marked initially by a new freedom from excessive authority, bleak conformity, and superfluous rules and regulations. The new community may be distinguished especially by its encouragement of self-motivation and self-expression. Some may live this freedom constructively. They become truly self-motivated and productive. For others the new liberty may be a source of laziness and inert conformity to anything that seems to be "in" at the moment. They surrender their newly gained freedom to a thoughtless identification with prevalent public reflexes. Soon the few who live creatively the new freedom for personal growth—clearly available to all—may become an unbearable reproach to the many who let the same possibility slip by. Collegiality and "community spirit" may then be abused by the many to level the few.

Thus the problem remains now and probably in the fu-

ture of how to live an original life. We have mentioned a
few unwise reactions, such as that of isolation, which is as
pernicious for the self-motivated man as for the people
around him. All he can try to do is to adapt his originality
to his concrete life situation, at least to some degree. We il-
lustrated this principle in our example of the style of generosity as lived in Italy and New England. We also told the
story of a volunteer for social work who went from the
United States to a small town in South America. In both
cases wise adaptation somehow changed the style of the
persons involved without robbing them of their uniqueness.
This adaptation made them more acceptable to others and
in no way forced them to betray themselves. What attitude
made it possible for them to change and still remain faithful
to their originality?

The people in both stories had one thing in common: a
loving respect for the people with whom they had to work
and live. It was this loving respect that made them eager to
know all they could about these people. Respect made them
sensitive to their nuances of thought, feeling, behavior. Out
of this loving awareness grew the recognition of how to be
their best selves among these people in spite of their differences in life motivation. This awareness on their part was
not theoretical. It was not gained from books or orientation
courses. Such means of instruction may have been helpful
as a first outline of what to do and how to be. But the real
thing happened on the spot. When they honestly tried to live
with the people in respectful empathy, they began to *feel*
what in their attitudes and behaviour would alienate them
unnecessarily from these people. Slowly their behavior responded to this newly emerging sensitivity. Without betraying what they were, they became more acceptable to their
fellow men. This road of loving respect undoubtedly is an
effective road for the self-motivated man to follow among
people who do not understand the particular expressions of
his originality. This respectful empathy can only emerge,

however, after identifying and solving faulty childhood reactions against people who may have made the exceptional person suffer cruelly as a youngster at home, in school or neighborhood.

Overcoming of Envy by Value Reverence

At the end of this chapter of detailed observation and advice in regard to the appearance of envy in our lives, it may be good to conclude with a more universal consideration of the way in which I can transcend envy.

Human life is not something I can manipulate at will. The futile attempt to manipulate life means I am forgetful of its mystery. Nonetheless I may be tempted to reduce the fullness of my humanity to only one of its necessary dimensions—that of functionality. No doubt, I must organize to some degree my functional endeavors. Many sciences assist me in this task—the medical, economic, behavioristic, and legal, to mention only a few. My deepest humanity, however, is like a window opening on to wider horizons. Human life implies the ability to surpass the everyday without leaving it behind or depreciating it. This ability can bring a certain dignity and splendor to even the most trivial occupations. Human life also enables me to look at myself or others with envy or respect. It is precisely my creative freedom as a human person that allows me to live my life in one or the other attitude.

What makes it possible for me to envy others is the interaction of two characteristics of man. First, as man I spontaneously appreciate human values. This appreciation gives me a spontaneous awareness of goodness, truth, and beauty; it makes me aware that I can only grow as a man when I participate in human values, when I make them real in my life. My whole being and becoming is dependent on my personal participation in values as they concretely appear in myself and my surroundings.

A second characteristic, however, interferes with my openness to values and makes envy a possibility. It is the fact that I am limited in my appreciation of values, for values necessarily appear to me in my finite historical and cultural situation. I am called to live values in a unique or limited way. What my limitation is depends on the innate restrictions of my basic personality and on the possibilities offered to me by my social and historical situation. No doubt I should daily expand my possibilities. This kind of improvement, however, is subjected to certain boundaries that I do not know in advance and that I can never discover in their totality. But there is no doubt that I can only do so much within my life span or within the life span of the few generations in whose development I am called to participate.

The structure of the human person implies, thus, that he can find peace only when he accepts himself as he is, namely as a limited person who cannot realize all values to the highest possible degree. He must reconcile himself with the fact that he can make his life worth while in certain areas but not in others.

A tension may develop between the two characteristics just described. On the one hand, I spontaneously appropriate values that I experience both as sustenance for my humanity and as immensely attractive. On the other hand, I feel condemned to concretize in my life only a unique or limited profile of values. There are certain values I cannot live; there are other values I cannot realize to the same degree as some people are able to realize them. Tension between the values I can realize in my life and those I can desire but not realize may lead to the emergence of envy in me.

Tension arises when I cannot accept my personal life calling. My life calling tells me how and to what degree I can live values best in terms of my concrete life situation. Envy emerges when I cannot accept my uniqueness or limits. I look spitefully on any realization of value that I myself cannot live. If envy had its way, it would destroy not only this value as lived by the other, but, if it could, the very value itself.

One can also view the opposite attitude of envy—respect —from the viewpoint of the two interacting characteristics of man just described. On the one hand, I spontaneously appreciate human value. On the other hand, I am called to realize only certain values in my life in a unique or distinctly limited way. Because of my spontaneous appreciation of values, I experience a natural surge of admiration and desire for goodness, truth, and beauty. I tend toward appreciation and reverence wherever and whenever I meet their manifestation. Originally, I feel attracted and drawn by values and I deeply desire to participate in them. This is the ground of respect.

People, events, and things only become valuable, however, in the *lived* experience of man. The manifestations of goodness, truth, and beauty in this world are dormant until man enjoys and reverences them. To respect is to bring to light the splendor of values hidden in myself, in others, and in my surroundings. My expression of respect and admiration for these values may help to remove the blinders from the eyes of others so that they too can see the hidden splendor of this world. It is this miracle of transfiguration that respect can perform among men. Respect is a precious gift from man to man. Man is the only place where goodness, truth, and beauty can reveal themselves. More than anything else, man ought to share with his fellow man the respect that reveals value as value.

Man himself is the value of values. The fact that he is the only one in this world able to experience goodness, truth, and beauty in a free and unique way constitutes his human dignity. It makes him fundamentally worthy of respect. Respecting myself and other men means allowing and promoting in man his capacity to embody uniquely those values that he is called to live in a unique or limited way. Respect makes me sensitive to any value potentially or actually present in the other or in myself. Often it is difficult to detect the faint traces of value that lie concealed under manifold human distortions and perversions. But respect enables me to look again and again, inspired by an unshakable faith that the human person is called to be a revelation of some value, no matter how small and hidden. Even under the cover of distortion, true respect is able to detect a glimpse of the search for goodness, truth, and beauty which man is.

Respect is thus rooted in my spontaneous appreciation of value. It extends itself secondarily to myself or others, as called to be limited living participations in the inexhaustible mystery of value from which all limited manifestations flow. My respect for unique or limited manifestations of value is rooted in their participation in value itself.

Respect is endangered when I separate my interest in a limited manifestation of value from my involvement in value as such. Value as value surpasses each of its temporal and local manifestations. My limited participation in value can become separated from my openness to value as value. When this happens, participation in value turns into sterile possession and manipulation of some isolated manifestation of value. I may find it more important that I possess, master, and manipulate value than that I truly participate in it.

Participation implies that I make value real in myself— but not as if I were an isolated container or carrier of that value. Value participation is my limited original manifestation of a value which I deeply experience as infinitely more than I myself can ever be. To participate implies respect; possessiveness is disrespect. Respect and admiration open me for that which is deeper, greater, and more mysterious than my part in it. What I possess in isolation loses its mystery. Possessive isolation severs me from life-giving participation in the mystery that surrounds and surpasses me. I try to reduce the infinite to my size.

Reducing value to mere possession, personal adornment,

or means of advancement means that it can no longer inspire awe. What I possess is no longer the living value itself, but a sterile manifestation of value that has lost contact with its nourishing ground. It is like an amputated part of a body or the cut-off branch of a tree. I can own the branch. I can do with it what I want. But soon it will lose its aliveness, wither, and die.

The attempt to accumulate values as if they were things leads to envy. I greedily eye values as something I can hoard; I am envious of those who hoard them more copiously than I. Envy thrives in a civilization that has lost communion with values as surpassing each one of its limited manifestations. Recapturing the original experience of respectful appreciation of values can cure envy. When I am able to restore my spontaneous appreciation of value as value, then I can welcome in respect and admiration the revelation of value no matter where it comes from or in whom it is manifested. I will no longer experience value in the other as his isolated possession which threatens my isolated possession. Rather I will respect value in him as a manifestation of the goodness, truth, and beauty in which I and all men are called to share in some way and to some degree. Then the value in the other becomes my nourishment and delight instead of the source of my spiteful look.

From this emerges the insight that true competition is based on shared respect for a specific value. Both parties esteem this value so highly that they try to outdo each other in their attempt to live this value. My rival may succeed better than I. However, I can still admire the way in which he brings to life the value I too admire so much. To be sure, I would have liked to participate in this value as well as he. While this defeat may temporarily diminish my satisfaction and prestige, it does not necessarily evoke envy or diminish my joy in the value itself. Never would I experience the value competed for as his or my exclusive possession. On the contrary, his success inspires me to do better the next time.

Chapter Four

Self-Motivation and Originality

Afraid to be myself, I may go along with the whims of people around me. Fear cripples. If you have ever had a nightmare, you know what I mean. You are driving a car. You gather speed. A child appears on the road. You press the brake. The car keeps speeding. You break out in cold sweat. In panic you feel that you can't stop the car. You are paralyzed. You wake up terrified. It takes time before you know it was only a dream. You no longer limp with fear; you dare to move.

Why can't I move when overcome by fear?

I am a child. Daddy tells me I should swim in the sea. He takes me there. I hesitate. I'm scared. He pleads with me; he pushes me. I am in the water. He shouts at me to strike out as he taught me at home. I don't dare to. I want to feel under my feet the safe, shallow ground near shore.

It is difficult to move when I feel that any move I make will get me in trouble. I move freely when I feel it's safe to do so. A swimmer who knows the sea, who trusts his own skill, strikes out; he dares to move. But a fearful man does not move easily into a dangerous spot. He has to move himself against his fear of what might happen to him. A demolition expert who has to defuse a bomb on the verge of explosion realizes, "One wrong move and I'll be blown to bits." His instinct is not to move at all or to run. He must force himself to do the job.

It demands effort to do something when crippled by fear. I do not want to fight my own misgivings. Yet I may have to move in spite of them. Or I may have to let myself be moved by others. Few soldiers would tackle the enemy if not moved forward by throngs of men. Few people would risk their lives in street fights if not carried along by irate crowds. A man in fear may give in to the goading of others.

At times only my body seems moved by people around me. A crowd of movie-goers may push me toward the street when the film is over. I go along with them without thinking about it. Often, however, I am involved in my moves inwardly. I feel that I am doing something for some reason. The swimmer who dives into a dangerous river may be moved by a desire to prove himself or by such motives as gaining strength, keeping fit, getting in shape for a contest. The man who disarms an explosive shell may want to save the life of others, look like a hero, or simply keep his job.

I may thus be moved by motives that are my own or by the motives of others. A boy who takes part in the mischief of a gang may not be moved by his own decisions. He is driven by the dictates of his pals.

Many of us are like the boys in the gang. Afraid to be the origin of our own motives, we let ourselves be moved by the tastes and the drives of an anonymous public. Secretly we feel ashamed about our betrayal of selfhood. We may envy the person who is propelled by his own initiative. He makes us aware of what is missing in us.

Self-Motivation Accompanied by Anxiety

Why does fear cripple self-motivation? Self-motivation originates in me. Others may stimulate me, but their stimulation works its way through my center. I weigh the evidence. I ask myself what it means to me. I come to a decision. Not the crowd, not somebody else, but I. Self-motivation is rooted in personal insight and choice. It is marked by originality.

To motivate myself originally, I must become aware of the meanings of my own life and of the people, events, and things around me. Once I know what something can mean to me, I can decide whether or not I want to be moved by this meaning. I can ask myself if my striving after this meaning would be in tune with what I am. Thus growth in self-motivation has to do with discovery of meaning.

An animal cannot be self-motivated; neither can it lead an original life or freely choose some meanings over others. Its instinctual make-up tells it once and for all what its environment means. The animal has a relatively fixed set of drives, needs, and instincts. Only certain aspects of its surroundings can arouse it. This arousal is obeyed blindly. There is no choice.

Our first ancestors, just emerging from pre-human life, were probably mainly moved by inner drive and tribal pressure. They could not foster a richly differentiated self-motivated life. Self-insight and self-motivation, while not totally absent, were probably at a minimum. Slowly, however, drive became more enlightened by insight. Self-orientation became more pronounced.

Self-orientation shapes my life. It moves me to do some things and omit others. Let's say my self-orientation is to be a musician. Early in life, I found the meaning of music for me. I felt I should be a pianist. To this meaning I committed myself. Since that day I have done all sorts of things to help me become a better pianist: I take lessons, go to concerts, practice daily, give recitals. Other things I avoid: work that may harm my hands, activities that would take me away from my practice, excessive socializing with people who do not share my interest.

The origin in me of all these do's and don'ts is a lasting

originating attitude. "Originating" because this attitude is the origin of specific self-motivated acts of mine. "Lasting" because it molds my life day by day. This attitude moves me constantly in a certain direction. Such a persistent and dynamic attitude, which is at the origin of specifically oriented actions, is a motivation.

Motivation is a lasting, originating self-orientation toward a certain meaning. For example, I may be attracted to another person in many ways. He has many meanings for me. I may see him as intellectually interesting, as a father who can protect me, as a person who can be my friend. I may see him as a teacher, counselor, or leader of men. Out of these many meanings, I choose one that he can have for me. Then I link my life to his within this specific meaning.

Let's say I choose to see him as an enlightened leader of men and decide to motivate myself to be one of his followers. This motivation becomes a lasting originating attitude in me. Orientation toward him as a leader becomes the origin of numerous acts of loyalty to him. To be sure, there is a blind drive in man to follow others. But in the case of self-motivation, this drive is enlightened by insight and freedom. I freely choose to follow a certain person within the limits of the meaning he has for me. I choose him because I have gained insight into his personality, his qualifications, the special charism of his leadership. I weighed all of this in relation to my personality and to my unique task and position in life. I pondered the pros and the cons. Finally I motivated myself to follow him. That motivation is an inner force which from now on will sustain and guide my unfolding as a person.

In motivation, drive thus becomes enlightened. Motivation is drive-transformed and directed by human insight and choice. Blind drive originates in nature. It originates in us as part of nature. However, it is our insightful self that is the origin of motivation or "enlightened drive." Such motivation in turn becomes the origin of a whole series of actions that tend to realize the chosen meaning or value in my life. My life will be shaped by them. I will be what my motivations are.

The history of humanization is the story of a transformation, the transformation of blind drive into human motivation. Blind drive originates in nature and crowd. Human motivation originates in the human self and human community. To the degree that motivation originates in the original self, it can be called self-motivation. In that case it is an affirmation and expansion of human originality.

Self-motivation is the dynamic growth, transformation, and expression of the latent originality of a person. When man develops self-motivations, he freely channels his drives in certain directions in tune with some of his unique possibilities and spontaneous inclinations. This development is accompanied by anxiety. Anxiety emerges at all decisive moments in which humanity or the human individual has to rise from drive to motivation or from one level of motivation to a new level.

To raise drive to motivation, I have to discover myself as the solitary responsible origin of what will move and shape my life in the future. Motivation is responsible drive. To find myself as origin is to distance myself from blind drive, crowd, and collectivity so that I may become a personal consciousness. Anxiety is the birth pang of a new awareness of self. This birth means separation from the womb of crowd and nature. Before that break, I was painlessly moved along by others, by my natural needs and instincts. I did not have to care personally where I was going. Such separation is accompanied by apprehension, for I suddenly find myself alone and responsible in a world that may neither understand nor appreciate what I am uniquely called to be and do.

The same kind of fear emerges again when I enter a new level of motivation, such as the motivation to marry, to become a political activist, to join a religion, or to dedicate my life to the study of ancient art. It is like being born again. I become the origin of a new originating self-orientation, and this always implies a risk, a venture into the unknown.

Often motivational development is stunted because people do not dare to take this step. A new motivation means that I discover a new value or an old value in a new way. I boldly decided to orient my life and behavior toward this value, no matter the risk or pain involved. Motivation places this newly discovered value at the center of my life.

A new self-motivation enlarges my originality. While still in tune with my unique potentiality, it is new insofar as it signals the expression of my uniqueness in a new life situation. The new motivation is the origin of a new direction; it becomes for me a source of decisions and actions. Life must now renew itself in line with this new value. I affirm this newly chosen value as one of my criteria for original self-unfolding.

For example, I become aware in a new way that blacks ought to have equal rights. I ask myself what this realization means for the kind of man I am. The subsequent insight may become for me a central motivation. In other words, I let this motivation come forth from my center or original self. I cannot say for sure where this motivation will lead. It may break up old patterns of life. It may even alienate me from family, friends, and neighbors. Therefore, my decision to motivate myself in this direction may be fraught with anxiety.

A therapist knows from experience the anxiety that can emerge in a client faced with the decision to originate a new motivation. The client is anxious because he realizes that he himself must decide on some new dynamic way of living that will definitely shape his future day by day.

Anxiety accompanies not only the motivational growth of the individual but that of culture and society as well. As a matter of fact, the motivation of individual members of a culture is never an isolated event; it is always rooted in a matrix of common motivations. Common motivation must in turn be personally appropriated by members of the community in order to remain a living motivation and not to deteriorate into blind drive or dead convention.

My personal motivations are sustained by the motivations that are alive in my society. I live these in my own way. Personal motivations are unique modulations of some freely selected common motivations. When my personal appropriation of a common motivation becomes minimal, it is no longer self-motivation but public motivation. When personal appropriation is totally absent, we cannot even speak of public motivation; public reflex takes its place.

Any invitation to appropriate a new motivation is bound to cause apprehension. A change of motivation implies a change of heart as well as a change in the usual way of doing things. Say that in a small southern town people have been motivated to look at blacks as secondary citizens. A change in this motivation means a change of heart, but this is not all. Motivation originates acts. Acts give rise to new situations. Before this, the motivation to patronize blacks originated a style of life, an economy, a distinct social stratification. This choice affected the life of every man in town. The new motivation to treat blacks as equals will necessarily originate a new style, a new economy, a new classification. The daily life of each man will be affected. Change of motivation may mean the disappearance of a familiar world.

An as yet unknown world of culture and action will arise from a new motivation. Most people will be touched by anxiety. Some will suffer more than others. They feel more responsible for the motivations chosen by their culture. A few may break down under this pressure. There are also those who lack originality. What is motivation for others is only social pressure for them. Since they did not reach or have lost the stage of self-motivation, they are not able to make their own the motivations that are alive in others.

At present, signs of motivation anxiety are everywhere

around us. We are constantly invited to reorient ourselves
anew, to change our tried and true ways.

Motivational Problems in Our Age

Today, I can in some measure reject society. I can isolate
myself from others whereas isolation would have meant suicide for primitive man. The more affluent society, the more
I can distance myself from it. Affluence enables me to keep
myself alive in relative loneliness. I can buy tools, appli-
ances, furniture, canned and frozen foods. Sustained by
these things, I can stay alive on the "island" of my apart-
ment for days.

Primitive man could not survive outside an almost constant togetherness with his fellow man. This was one of the
reasons he did not spontaneously develop the motivation
to live a more private existence. He could not choose to
live more inside or more outside of his society, but I can,
and this possibility is a source of anxiety. I can map out my
future in some divergence from my fellow men. As a result,
I feel more alone in my responsibility for my choice and its
possible consequences. I may feel anxious because of the
risk such choosing entails.

Primitive man was inclined to accept nature in its given-
ness. He did not reshape it more than necessary. He was
satisfied with the minimum structuring of nature necessary
for survival. He would build simple huts, fashion elementary tools and weapons. He did not feel compelled as modern
man does to utilize to the utmost the powers of nature.

Modern society sets out to create a world of its own. Decisions have to be made in regard to the type of world that
seems best for man. Nature and society are to be shaped in
certain ways and not in others. We must choose to be motivated to some types of common action and not to others.
We know that the kind of action we choose will make a certain kind of world. The question is what kind of world? This

question evokes anxiety. We are not sure in advance what kind of civilization will lead us to self-creation or to self-annihilation. Some forfeit the choice and the anxiety that goes with it. They grope along as anonymous public men, satisfied to live with choices made by others.

Anxiety emerges in regard to such things as development of destructive weapons, automation, environmental controls, the influence of techniques on the education of the young. Faced with such decisions, apprehension is inevitable. The freer man becomes from nature and the further he grows in the life of self-orientation, the heavier the burden of his anxiety. He has to choose what the world will be like and risk the consequences of his choice. The history of humanization is a history of liberation from nature. It is thereby also a history of increase in the possibilities for anxiety. Thus some choose the easy way out: surrender to the public reflex does not incite the motivation to make a new world but neither does it evoke anxiety.

Anxiety has accompanied man from the first moment of his emergence. Primitive tribes were open to anxiety too. They could not master frightening events in nature scientifically. They relied on magic. Magic belief was an effective balm against certain fears. It reduced some of their problems to one formula: either I succeed in placating the gods or I don't. There is not much else I can do. Once I have tried to do so, it is useless to worry much more. Things will happen anyway as the gods decree after judging the tribal rites.

Modern scientific man, while he may have a magic of his own, is beyond the magic of the primitive. He knows more about the powers that endanger life and society. He believes that the enemies of human life can be subdued. He has, sciences, laboratories, technical facilities, organization. At the same time, he is aware that scientific knowledge and technique are limited. These limits make him fearful, but his fear cannot be quelled by magic rites. A surgeon in a deli-

cate operation is more anxious than a witch doctor. Magic
thinking made the medicine man fatalistic about the outcome of his practice. The price the surgeon pays for insight
and freedom is anxiety. The low level of motivational development kept primitive man free from the development
of certain possibilities of anxiety that are familiar to us. Thus
there seems to be a correlation between the possibilities for
anxiety and the development of motivation.

Anxiety seems to emerge at certain moments of our motivational life. We say motivational *life* to stress the dynamic
aspect of human motivation. The term "motivation" may
suggest a motionless thing, a piece of equipment set up in
our "inner" lives. In reality, motivation is man's personal
moving with others in the world. Motivation makes it possible for man to actualize himself in ever-new ways. True
motivation is always deepening, expanding, and differentiating itself.

Motivation is first of all a dynamic orientation toward
values. Secondly, it is a dynamic orientation toward acts
and actions that can realize these values. The motivating
value appears to man in constantly changing situations. He
thus has to decide to motivate himself to new courses of
action. He has to choose what kind of action can actualize
the value motivating him in a given situation.

A man marries a woman out of love. He makes her personal value one of the sources of his life motivation. He
says to himself that her well-being will be one of the meanings that will motivate his actions. He soon discovers that
the promotion of her happiness may take a variety of forms.
They change with the diversity of situations in which he and
his wife find themselves. He gradually learns the kinds of
things he should do if he wants to serve the well-being of
his wife concretely.

This example shows how a life motivation differentiates
itself spontaneously into many detailed motivations. These
in turn strengthen, deepen, and make more real the funda-

mental motivation from which they sprang. Such growth and differentiation continues as long as one's originality stays alive as an originating force.

Already it has been made clear that the anxiety that accompanies motivation can emerge whenever I choose a new motivation. Now we can see why anxiety also appears with each new differentiation of an old or new motivation that remains fundamentally the same. Every new situation—related to my former choice—puts me in a dilemma. Either I am disloyal to my chosen motivation, or I have to differentiate this same motivation in accordance with the demands of the moment. I cannot know for sure how to differentiate my motivation in the wisest way. Different courses of action are open to me. I always risk a wrong decision. I am anxious, moreover, because I must give up some certitude. I must risk a new differentiation of my existing motivation. I must decide on a new modulation of this motivation, one which has not yet proved to be effective. Therefore, I cannot keep my motivational life alive and differentiating if I cannot bear with uncertitude and apprehension.

The development of motivation entails the wise expansion and realistic differentiation of human originality in tune with the times. The pace of scientific and technological discovery confronts man with problems he would not have dreamed of a century ago. He must constantly ponder how to realize in modern life his original motivations. Every decision to differentiate motivation is likely to be accompanied by anxiety and, as we shall see, the occasions for motivational anxiety today exceed anything man has known in the past.

Complexity of Modern Life and Its Effects on Motivation

The world vision of contemporary man is wide open. Far from being a closed and final structure, the world is experienced as an ever-expanding horizon of possibilities. Every new empirical finding, even when answering some of man's questions, opens up an overwhelming number of new problems.

As we have said, anxiety emerges when man must motivate himself in a new way in response to newly discovered values. Today we are bombarded by new intimations of truth that disrupt our lives and free us to revolutionize our motivational systems.

At the start of this era, modern man began to experience accelerated and complicated transitions on the scientific, political, economic, and industrial scene. His situation was like that of the adolescent who moves out of familiar surroundings and traditional certainties. The adolescent starts to explore life for himself. He is no longer satisfied with the image of the world handed down to him by authorities. He wants to experience for himself what life is like, to see with his own eyes, hear with his own ears, understand with his own mind.

The world seems different from what the adolescent believed it to be. Life is not what he expected. The world view in which he was immersed as a child breaks down. His naïve trust in the traditional image of the world gives way to distrust. If this cherished image proves untrue, how can he be sure that all other dimensions of life will not undergo the same fate?

The adolescent moves into a set of motivations quite different from what motivated him before. He feels moved to question his childish view of the world. He also questions those whom he feels are responsible for his vision of life: authority, tradition, conventions handed down from generation to generation. He feels that his ties with family, cultural background, community are loosening up. This development is accompanied by excitement and anxiety. The opening up of unexpected vistas prompts feelings of conquest, adventure, elation, fascination. At such moments the adolescent feels motivated to live a new and exciting life, no matter the

in the eyes of her neighbors and, more important, what role it may play in the future of her child. If Mary is so much faster and obviously more clever than Johnny, then she may not only look better to the neighbors but also her future may be brighter than Johnny's. She may even feel that she as a mother may look less good because her child is not as clever as the neighbor's. This feeling too may be projected into the future in terms of ambitious fantasies about the achievements of the child. Once he makes good, the parents will look good—or so they think.

Instead of looking at values themselves, we look at the degrees of success they promise us in the competitive society. If a child of ours would have an asset that does not assure social esteem, we may underestimate that gift. For example, a child may show early in life a spontaneous propensity for solitude and recollection. This rare gift—not to be confused with an inability to relate to others—may prepare him for a life of unusual wisdom, peace, and harmony. But this is the kind of asset that will not necessarily endear him to agitated neighbors, to aggressive brothers or excitable playmates in the street. Measured against the scale of social success, this bent toward solitude may be seen as a deficiency rather than an asset. Comparison inspired by concern for social success may blind us to certain values.

We can now see more clearly how a child can be initiated early into a life of odious comparison. When mother tells Johnny about the success of others, anxiousness creeps into her voice. She makes Johnny feel that it would be nice if he would do as well or even better, even if it is impossible for him to do so. He begins to sense that his worth depends on how well he measures up against the social success of Mary. Johnny may become estranged from his unique self. He may, even at this early stage, begin to strive after a life that can never be his. He interiorizes mother's look of odious comparison, which will lead to envy. The same attitude destroys or diminishes his ability for gratitude.

Gratitude is the joyful acknowledgment of original gifts in ourselves and others that cannot be deserved. Gratitude is the recognition that undeserved gifts in ourselves and others are means of gratuitous enrichment for all. Gratitude is a form of respect, the opposite of envy. As long as we live in gratitude, it is impossible to be envious. The death of gratitude in modern society means the birth of envy as a prevailing force. Comparing myself constantly with others along the lines of social success blinds me for values in themselves. Values go far deeper than social success that they may or may not provide; they grant me a far more lasting joy.

My experience of social eminence is usually based on comparison with others less successful than I. To make this comparative self-experience the basis of my happiness is precarious. I am always in danger of meeting other people socially better off than I, no matter how well I have done up to this moment. If my happiness is built merely on being more successful than others socially, it will cave in like a house of cards the moment I meet others more eminent.

Modern society is a changing society. The factors that make people socially eminent change fast. There was a time when people with a facility for setting up their own business enjoyed eminence. Then there came the era of large companies when people who were naturally polished and co-operative could grow to prominence. Soon a combination of inventiveness and co-operation may grant social eminence to executives in new industries that demand both independence and conciliation.

When such changes take place, people whose gift was popular and sought after in a former period may lose their status and position. If they appreciated more the accidental benefits of their gifts than the gifts themselves, they may feel despondent or bitter and end up as envious men and women.

The initiation into a life of envious comparison started in Johnny's home. It may have been continued in his school. The school in its modern form teaches children to compare themselves with other children. They do so not in terms of each one's unique gift. The teachers may compare them mainly on the basis of certain successes that go with one-sided intellectual or technical capacities. A school may be a breeding place for envy. This is not surprising. A school tends to represent the values of the society for which it is preparing people. The consumer society needs to play on envy for the selling of goods and services that promise people that they will be as well or better off than others. The productive society needs envy to incite people to work harder for the acquisition of higher positions and bigger rewards that prove to them that they are more clever or have exerted themselves better than their neighbors.

The school may help to instill the spirit of odious comparison which is the soul of an envious civilization. The children are made to feel that they succeed by their own force or cunning. The successful ones easily become conceited. They are always comparing themselves with others. Their happiness depends a great deal on how well they find themselves doing in comparison with their peers—a precarious existence indeed.

The longer education takes, the more entrenched the student may become in the spirit of comparison. Objective examinations, for instance, cannot really measure the original gifts of a person. Some of these gifts are measured to a degree, of course. But what is measured mainly are the isolated skills and the exertion of the student independent of his deepest human originality. In an objective examination, he proves how well he has mastered certain subjects his materialistic society wants him to master almost exclusively. He experiences this success in the school as his own doing. There is little room for creativity in the life of the average student. A person who, on the contrary, does something that wells up from his original undeserved gifts may feel humble and grateful. He may realize that the source of his performance is not his own doing. He may experience his gift as gift—not a gift that he has but a gift that he is.

Simply being the person I am is to live in grateful loyalty to the gift that I am. At such moments, I do not live in odious comparison. What I uniquely am is incomparable. Otherwise it would not be unique.

Gratitude for Values in Others

The more I become aware of my uniqueness as gift, the more I will be able to appreciate the uniqueness of my fellow men too. I begin to live in a spirit of gratitude. I live in humble acknowledgment of the undeserved gifts that in various ways and measures are given to different people. Something peculiar happens to my life experience. I come to feel deeply that the personal gift of each person points to a realm of value that surpasses each one of us. Spiritual values are incarnated in concrete persons. These values do not become their property. These persons do not own their personal originality as they own a bicycle, a new car, a bookcase, or a French poodle. They truly are these personal values but they are so by participation.

If, for instance, generosity or wisdom could be totally identified with some generous or wise person, then there would be no generosity or wisdom left for others. This is clearly not the case. Each unique person is only a limited participation in universal values. In gratitude, I can fully appreciate the manifestation of value in another. In some cases this manifestation may become for me an appeal, a summons, an invitation to live this same value in my life.

I do not feel, however, that I am dependent on the person whose life becomes an appeal to me. I experience that the value itself is far more than its incidental and temporal manifestation in his life. I may even realize how he himself often fails to be loyal to the value he is called to live. I never identify this value with the person as such. The self-motivation of the other was first a stimulus coming from the outside. When I began to respond to it, I became aware that my innermost being was touched by his example. My given originality awakened and began to endow this stimulus with a special personal meaning. It became a summons for me from which I did not hide. I was filled with a feeling of gratitude and respect.

The appeal to my uniqueness was not simply an invitation to copy blindly this person's life. It was felt as the appeal of a higher realm of values of which he was only the temporary manifestation, speaking to me through his concrete life about things that go beyond both of us.

The same may happen in relation to persons and events in history. Historical science can deteriorate into a monstrous filing system of dates and deeds. Documentation is useful and should by no means be neglected. But we should not lose sight of the fact that history is more than an accumulation of facts. There can also be a history of splendid self-motivations in which the original selves of heroes, saints, and wise men are shown to be drawn out by eternal values in specific historical situations. To learn these moments of greatness, to dwell upon them, can have the same effect as my dwelling in the nearness of a highly motivated person in my surroundings.

We may be inspired by the motivations of a Lincoln, a Kierkegaard, an Einstein, a Hammarskjöld, or a Mme. Curie, even if such persons are only known to us through history. Biographies of great men can have the same impact. It is even not necessary that the stories of great persons be factual history. Legends can do as well or better. A legend can be the embodiment of a great and moving motivation transposed into a human interest story. This story may have developed as a result of the impression a great person made on his contemporaries. They were sensitive to the summons of value hidden in his life. To celebrate that appeal, they enriched and deepened his story. They made it greater than life. In so doing, they were inspired by the fact that the value represented by a person is greater than any one person himself.

How important it is to expose ourselves to history as appeal. We can enlarge our possibilities for the awakening of our innermost originality. The story becomes greater than the man. But the value celebrated is still immeasurably greater than the story.

Dwelling and Original Living

To grow in originality, I have to live in respect and gratitude. I have to be present to values in self and others, in life and nature. This means being present without distortion by envious comparison, by unwarranted concern for public opinion and social appearance. Then I overcome the sting of envy in myself. I also go beyond the leveling impact of envious comparisons made by others. I move in the world in a new way. How can this movement be described—this original, gracious, noncomparative movement toward human values, this movement filled with respect? Perhaps we could best describe it as a movement of dwelling.

Dwelling means to allow life to reveal itself to me in any way it chooses to do so. "Dwelling" is a metaphorical expression. It alludes to a certain style of human movement in a landscape. I dwell in the woods; my mood and orientation are different when I drive to office or supermarket. Dwelling is aimless and yet deeply meaningful. Relaxed posture and movement reveal my liberation from the tense attention that marks my behavior as I fight my way through traffic jams to reach my office on time. Yet there is no absence of attention when I am dwelling. I experience a peaceful attentiveness that makes me aware of meanings I tend to overlook in daily life.

I smell with delight trees and flowers; I look in wonder at swans floating on a lake that shimmers before me. A beautiful young deer may captivate my attention for a superb moment as it stands in perfect stillness among firs and evergreens. I catch my breath as the deer turns and leaps away in graceful agility.

Moments like these are most impractical. My perceptions, thoughts, and feelings seem to leave their well-trodden pathways as I dwell in the woods. Life is experienced anew in light of what I see, touch, and smell. I sense deeper meanings; I begin to ask questions which I may not ask in working hours. Spontaneously I begin to originate a world of meaning and value as countless others have done before me. This dwelling in the woods is a symbol and expression of a far deeper dwelling that takes place within me.

Another example of the dwelling attitude can be seen in an incident of dwelling on dramatic masterpieces. A so-called "Laboratory Theater" was started by Jerry Grotowski in 1959. Eight unknown actors and this young director of only twenty-six came together to form a company in a provincial town in Poland. One of the distinctive features of this theater is its interest in bringing to life classical drama, poems, myths, and parables. Director and actors dwell on the living message of this literature. They assimilate it personally. The classical drama is experienced in a way that is at the same time contemporary and unique for each one of the actors. New theatrical forms originate spontaneously from this dwelling experience; they try to express as simply and vividly as possible what they have felt while abiding with the dramatists of the past. Grotowski wants his actors not simply to memorize the texts of the masters but to confront them: they should struggle with their hidden meaning by abiding with them. The outcome of this personal confrontation is a creative rearrangement of the plays, together with the addition of new scenes and dialogues, without betraying their original lasting message.

The main way in which Grotowski achieves his results is by dwelling on the original scripts. A gifted actor participates

so intimately in the experience of the author that it becomes
his own experience. He is able to embody it originally in his
body and voice. The motivation of the heroes of the drama
become his self-motivation as he communicates the age-old
message to present-day audiences. Through constant dwelling, the message becomes so alive in the actor that he can
even abandon certain external settings. As Grotowski says,
the actor must be poor in the theatrical sense: he must be
able to fascinate his audience even without artifacts such as
make-up, props, costumes. If the actor has truly become at
home with the play, he is able to become an original expression for his contemporaries of the motives that motivated
the persons created by the playwright.

What is true for the actor can be true for the person asked
to dwell on the works of those who have given expression to
the original experiences of our common humanity in philosophy, poems, paintings, novels, sculpture, and music. The
average person may not be able to create these meanings
as impressively as does the actor or artist. Nevertheless he
too can assimilate the works of others and originate them
personally if he dwells continuously—like the actors in
Grotowski's company—on the monuments of human experience offered to him by humanity. Such experience is not
bound to one or the other specific culture. I don't have to
be a Greek of the eleventh century B.C. to appreciate the
experiences described by Homer in the *Iliad* and the
Odyssey.

Universal human motivations may be expressed by composers, sculptors, painters, poets, philosophers, and spiritual
masters. They may create classics that appeal to educated
people in other cultures as well as in their own. Bach,
Beethoven, and Mozart can thrill an Eastern audience educated to hear them. The same is true for a Westerner attend-
ing Japanese *Noh* plays or reading Confucius.

Deep human experiences are evoked by the creative expression of what the artist, poet, painter, or thinker has lived

personally. Their communication reverberates in the depths of my personality. Their expressions come to life for me. Such gifted men are able to express an original awareness of human life because they fostered in their own lives some solitude and recollection.

Here a mysterious dimension of originality confronts me: when most alone, I am most with others. I experience my deepest oneness with the other when I experience our common humanity in solitude. Out of this depth, I may be able to meet the other in spite of our differences. I experience the other as a unique manifestation of the humanity we share.

This originality goes deeper than the inventiveness of the man who shapes new cultural forms. Homer is immortal and universal not because he invented new ways of using language. That too is an element of his greatness. But he is a classic because he combined with his inventive genius for words the power to give shape in these words to universal human motivations he lived through inwardly.

Growth in originality can begin at home, continue from nursery school through graduate school, and beyond to everyday life. It means exposure to cultural creations that represent the depth and width of original human motivations—an exposure adapted to the age, background, and potentialities of the person. This education may begin in the family. The child awakens to wonder in fairy tales, melodies, and catchy rhymes. These imaginative flights allow him to experience life poetically before he is compelled to live it practically. While practical approaches are necessary, they should never become the exclusive way of meeting the mystery of life.

Wonder and Curiosity

At the heart of dwelling is the mood of wonder. Wonder differs from curiosity. Scientific and practical curiosity are necessary. If curiosity is one-sidedly fostered, however, the sense of wonder may die. This is unfortunate. Originality is evoked only when we meet life in wonder and respect. It is difficult to speak about wonder. It is more than mere feeling, thinking, willing, and attentiveness. Wonder implies them all while going beyond them. Wonder is openness. I am open when not complicated by public opinion or envious comparison, by ambitions, anxieties, and passions. Wonder does not plan its course. It is a readiness to abide by any value that may present itself originally to me. It is found in children before its edge is taken off by education. Wonder leads to original knowledge.

Original knowledge grows like an organism. It assimilates to itself what it is ready to receive and what is consistent with the uniqueness of the knowing person. What I experience and assimilate in wonder is that which ties in with my original humanity. I can appropriate only what I in my uniqueness can receive at this special moment of my life.

We ought to say something also about sedimentations of originality. Each original dwelling in the world in wonder may add organically a new layer of experience and motivation to man's original being. There are also layers of information in the person. They are the result not of wonder but of man's informational attitude, of his scientific and practical curiosity. Sediments of information, if they remain mere information, are not likely to be interwoven with my uniqueness as a person. They are superimposed. They do not touch or make manifest my deepest inner core. I need information to protect and maintain daily life and to nourish my life of reflection. But this knowledge is very different from the intimate communion with values that is the result of wonder, the pristine knowing that sustains and expresses my deepest humanity. Wonder should thus be distinguished from curiosity. Both have their place in life. One cannot be substituted for the other.

The Anatomy Lesson of Dr. Tulp is a famous painting by Rembrandt. He had seen medical students and professors dissecting cadavers. Rembrandt shows us these men at work. The corpse is opened up. Our curiosity about anatomy makes us look with interest at this picture. If this scene, however, would merely satisfy our curiosity, it would not touch us deeply. But the painting may also make us wonder. We may sense the mystery of life and death, the meaning of man, the sacredness of life, the marvel of man's exploring look into what conditions his existence.

A boy may be curious about girls. He wants to know how they feel about things. What about their personality, their sexual life? He may date wildly, read books, or frequent movies which promise him more information. All this seems to change when he falls in love. The sublime moment of love is not marked by avid curiosity, even though curiosity may play a meaningful role. Love is filled with wonder. Love is not about what I can measure by comparison, tests, and questionnaires. Love is about the person as person, in all her mystery.

A man loves his wife because she is she. He does not love her because of one or the other quality he admires in her. In love he is in wonder about the mystery of the beloved. Wonder opens him to that mystery; it allows him to be a part of it. He can never know the other totally in her mystery. He can only grow in wonder and knowledge toward her and while so doing expand his own humanity. This wonder never dies; it remains alive forever.

Curiosity can be satisfied. To maintain it beyond satisfaction would bore me. The store of information which marriage partners can gain about one another may soon be exhausted. Without wonder, they may become bored. The sense of wonder that accompanies true love never leads to boredom; it makes people marvel about one another indefinitely.

Dwelling and wonder thus sustain and nourish each other. Wonder is the source and inspiration of my dwelling presence. Self-motivation becomes my progressive, original articulation of what I experience in wondering presence. Unlike the search for information, the movement of dwelling is marked by lack of precise direction. The young lover dwells in enchanted wonder with his beloved and in this rich moment shares the mystery of her being. Dwelling in wonder, we sense meanings and values we can never master or exhaust. We experience their content more as approaching us than as the outcome of our approach to them. We may receive their messages at moments we cannot predict in advance.

Every experience of wonder implies a deepening awareness of the whole of life and its meaning. Wonder is all encompassing. This is one of the reasons why wonder can never be satisfied, why it is pervaded by a vague restlessness. When I open myself in love and wonder to a person, I open up to that in him which manifests the original ground in which we all share. Wonder makes me aware of the fundamental originality of life. It reveals my human need to participate in this mystery.

Man as participant in the mystery of life and nature lives in wonder. Man as manipulator of his environment, as the controller of the biosocial condition of his life, lives in scientific and practical curiosity, which involves him in the serious search for relevant information. Information helps me to control my life situation to some degree. It tells me how to take care of my needs. Curiosity is motivated by the need for mastery. This may not be evident at first glance. But if I carefully look at what motivates my curiosity, I will find that in some way I hope to satisfy it for the sake of need fulfillment, protection, promotion, entertainment, efficient organization, and so on. My curiosity also gives me a kind of power over others insofar as I ferret out details about their life and work.

Curiosity is not only connected with control but can itself be controlled. I can evoke and maintain curiosity in myself and others by certain methods. A good teacher stimulates curiosity in students. An accomplished educator knows how to hold their attention and get his information across. These devices work well in the necessary informational education. They are useless in an education to originality.

Wonder is beyond manipulation. It is an experience that overwhelms and inspires a person. The educator cannot evoke it at will any more than a painter can evoke at will a new painting. No educator can compel an original experience. He can only bide his time. The "happening" of wonder in the student is a gift not a trick. Biding his time should not be understood as doing nothing. Biding should be an abiding.

The teacher helps the student make his abode among the creations of artists, thinkers, and writers. In their own good time they may evoke in the student an original sense of wonder. He can sustain the student in his abiding with the wealth of value offered by the past and present masters of human experience. He must not allow the student to delude himself into believing that information alone provides lasting entrance to the life work of great masters. Only the moment of wonder, which comes as gift, awakens the student to original value.

Education to wonder and education to curiosity, let us repeat, are both necessary. The former helps man to dwell among the original values and meanings he shares with humanity. The latter enables him to keep informed about matters that will help him maintain and enhance the biosocial underpinnings of human life and culture, of dwelling itself.

Closed and Open Curiosity

Curiosity is necessary. It becomes harmful only when it takes the sense of wonder away. Curiosity should not become so absorbing that it leaves no room for wonder. The curiosity that kills wonder is a closed curiosity. Open curiosity is guided by the awareness that the information one wants to obtain has a limited value.

Closed curiosity makes its object absolute. When I live in closed curiosity, I may believe, for example, that scientific research alone can disclose all the values and meanings needed to advance my life. Then I will not be inclined to go beyond this kind of knowledge. The sense of wonder will not easily emerge.

Present-day civilization needs well-informed men and women. Their wealth of information helps us to maintain the practical structures of society. Culture, therefore, rightly fosters a high regard for the informational attitude. However, many may come to believe that collections of scientific and factual data represent the highest wisdom of life. Because of this belief, they may bypass the wisdom that emerges in wonder. How many technicians of the biosocial underpinnings of life may never enjoy the deeper and lasting values life has to offer? A culture that cultivates only a closed curiosity will necessarily fail.

The wisdom given in wonder should enlighten curiosity. This wisdom makes us realize that the infrastructures of human life are not ends but means. They are meant to make us free for the superstructures of human living.

We should maintain instead an open curiosity—a curiosity that keeps us inquisitive while we remain deeply aware that its fruits are relative in comparison to those of original wisdom. This open curiosity will not diminish the search for information. Such information is necessary; it enables man to create a situation of freedom—the freedom to dwell originally in the world. Personal originality ought to inspire the avid curiosity that spurs man on to keep informing himself about how to create better conditions for dwelling in the world of meaning and value. An open curiosity will not lessen inquisitiveness; it will quiet the impetuousness that tends to make the search for information ultimate.

Convention and Originality

Two needs seem opposed to one another: the need to live
by the conventions of society; the need to make these conventions personal by living them in my own fashion. I must
share certain customs with my fellow men yet go beyond
them.

To give a simple example: a child learns to write like other
children. Yet after some time his writing begins to show personal features. He tells something about himself in his script.
Some people like to write in a mechanical way. They imitate
for a lifetime the models given to them in elementary school.
They repress any personal element; who they are does not
shine through in their writing. It is difficult even for an expert to read their personality from the flow and form of
their words.

I should live conventions in such a way that they become
an expression of what I personally am. To be original is to
be in motion, alive, and flexible. Therefore my original living of conventions ought to deepen in accordance with the
evolvement of my personality. I should see the customs of
my culture as occasions to discover and live out the dictates
of my originality.

Let's take another example, that of the handshake. In the
beginning of our culture, people who met tried to assure one
another that they could be trusted. They did so by showing
an open hand. Each one could see that no weapon was concealed. Soon the show of an open hand came to mean trust.
This custom became our familiar handshake. When shaking
hands, a person may express his trust in another human
being as well as other personal characteristics. Handshakes
may be distrustful, indifferent, formal, cordial, comforting,
sensual, wavering, or weak.

Conventions will remain dead for me as long as I do not
enliven them with my originality. I should rejoice in their

resurrection. However, once-dead customs should not be expected to come to life overnight. Some may be so far removed from our present-day experience that they cannot be brought to life at all. From time to time new customs have to be invented.

Conventional Wisdom and Original Discretion

A special kind of convention can be found in the conventional wisdom by which people try to live their lives meaningfully within the frame of the culture, country, and institutions to which they belong. To harmonize originality with this conventional wisdom is a special challenge.

Originality means personal responsibility. As a self-motivated man, I am faced in every new situation with the question: "What am I to do here and now to remain loyal to what I am?"

The conventional wisdom of the different societies to which we belong may guide us in our responses. Still, these guiding conventions are quite general. They certainly do not give us all the answers. Often they tell us only what we as human beings should not do; the question may still arise: "What ought I to do as the unique person I am?"

Respect, for example, is recommended by conventional wisdom. It implies that I do not hurt people. But how am I, with my temperament and background, with my responsibility and reputation, to make my respect concrete in relation to this particular person who always tries to take advantage of my kindness and pokes fun at my politeness? It is precisely in this here and now that I must live uniquely. How shall I respond wisely in tune with my originality, which conditions the uniqueness of each situation in which I find myself? Original discretion tries to answer this question in each new set of circumstances.

A first condition for original discretion is insight. I must try to understand who I am, what it means for me to be my true self individually and in unique relation to others and my surroundings. I must grow in the understanding of my life in all its movements and dimensions—in my family and neighborhood, in the institutions to which I belong, in my places of labor and leisure.

This insight implies that I must be aware of the conventional wisdom of my culture as a whole and of those institutions within my culture to which I have freely committed myself, be it as member of a family, church, social or professional organization, ideological movement, or charitable association. In this way I come to appreciate various styles in which I can live such motivating values as comradeship, respect, gratitude, graciousness, solitude, wonder, admiration, compassion, commitment, and truthfulness. Enlightened by this conventional wisdom, I come to know in general how I should act in tune with my human and cultural originality.

Still, there remains the crucial question: "How do I, as a unique person, bring this human and cultural wisdom to bear in my concrete situation here and now?"

I am Dr. Peterson, a research scientist in biochemistry, a man of precarious health and shy disposition. I learned recently about people in my city who suffer from malnutrition. I am invited to volunteer daily as part of a team to distribute food among them and to relieve their mood with pleasant and witty conversation. How am I to know what is the best thing for me to do here and now? I am neither terribly witty nor pleasant. Neither am I very handy in the distribution of things. Ironically, I need to devote all my time, attention, and energy to a breakthrough in the laboratory which may help solve the problem of chronic malnutrition by the composition of a potent nutrient that can be mass-produced cheaply. It will be of help not only for those who are underfed in my city but also for countless people all over the world. Should I get involved in local social service with all the distractions it might entail for my work? Or is my best

service to forgo conspicuous direct service to the poor so
that I may serve them best indirectly by preparing a scientific
solution for their malnutrition problem? Should I confine
myself to my laboratory and run the risk of being damned
as an ivory-tower scientist? Or should I perhaps engage
in a token service, such as distributing food on Tuesdays
only?

Evidently I need more than general conventional wisdom
to decide. It does not give me the concrete answers that I
need in the actual unique situation of my personal life. Conventional wisdom gives me a general orientation as to what
I ought to do, but inevitably it is up to me to decide what is
best in the here-and-now situation. This decision will involve
my unique personality as well as the people, conditions,
and possible consequences that are related to my personal
possibilities and deficiencies.

What should *I* do? This is the critical question each self-
motivated man asks himself. It is a question of original discretion.

Original discretion is an attitude that helps me to make my
self-motivations actual and concrete. It is an attitude that
moves me to make actual and real, through concrete acts,
what the demands of the moment ask for, in light of my loyalty to my original humanity as increasingly expressed in
my self-motivations.

How do I come to a decision by original discretion? It has
already been said that I must steep myself both in conventional wisdom and in assessment of myself and of the life
situation in which this universal wisdom has to be realized
concretely. While the acquisition of universal insight is a
necessary condition for original discretion, it is not its main
object or concern.

The primary field of interest for original discretion is my
concrete situation in all its uniqueness. Its purpose is not to
discover the general principles of conventional wisdom.
Original discretion presupposes those principles. Its concern

is to realize them originally in daily life. It takes its departure from a given situation as related to my uniqueness and attempts to examine all the aspects that may be relevant to the original stand to be taken.

To take another example, what is the right thing for a person like myself to do in regard to this student at this time? He has always applied himself in my courses and seminars. But now he is obstreperous; his remarks are insulting. He reacts to me in this manner because I refused to fall for his attempts to entrap me by idolizing my person and my lectures. It would have been bad for both of us if I had played the all-knowing, perfect idol or the doting daddy he wanted me to be. If I do not allow him in my next seminar, he may be so bitter that he begins to do badly in all his classes. Yet my personal sensitivity is such that his emotional opposition affects my peace of mind, my power of concentration, my verbal delivery. I am less effective. Being the person I am, I become strained and nervous. My whole seminar suffers from this. On the other hand, is it perhaps possible to discover unknown resources in myself? Maybe I will be able to overcome this inner disturbance so that it no longer affects my teaching. If I am able to bear with his presence in equanimity and put him in his place calmly, I may grow as a person. But am I not indulging in wishful thinking? Maybe my original gift does not contain these resources. Maybe it is far better for the person I am, and therefore for this student and for my class as a whole, that I do not allow him in my next seminar. Maybe I am so aggravated by his recalcitrance that my contact with him does him more harm than good. Perhaps the kindest thing for him and me is to create some distance between us. All these factors and perhaps many more, plus general conventional wisdom, have to be considered.

Original discretion presupposes knowledge of my original personality and knowledge of conventional human wisdom. It brings self-knowledge and conventional knowledge to bear

on the situation in which I find myself so that my original
humanity can be responsibly expressed in the actual decisions I make. Original discretion thus deals with concrete actions in terms of my response to my originality and its
prolongation in a unique set of self-motivations. My judgment about meeting the demands of the moment is made in
terms of my fundamental life decision to live concretely what
I am called to be originally.

Evidently, then, such discretion must be enlightened by
loving trust in my original calling and relaxed acceptance of
my manifold limitations. It must be reinforced by loving
respect for what I basically am. This by no means implies
that I will violate the rights of others. On the contrary, the
care for others is part of the demands of my original humanity. My uniqueness is only a personal modulation of these
universal demands.

For example, if I am called to be a reflective thinker, I
may ultimately serve my fellow men best by faithfulness to
solitude; called to be a social leader, I may serve them best
by being where the action is. The care for humanity is the
same, its expression is different. Both the demand to care
and the demand to embody that care in a unique style of life
and service are rooted in my original humanity.

Another aspect of original discretion is that it is continuously operative, though I may not be aware of it most of the
time. It is in more complex or trying circumstances that I
become aware that I am seeking to act with original discretion. Thus, for instance, if an acquaintance asks me to drive
him home and I am able and free to do so, I usually respond
without much thought. In such uncomplicated incidences of
everyday life, original discretion is at work, but quickly,
flexibly, spontaneously, out of a lasting self-motivation that
applies to this kind of situation. On the other hand, the fellow who asks for a ride may be a cunning operator who always tries to impose his companionship on me so that he may
use my acquaintanceship and my name for his own purposes.

His personality, manners, and principles are so at odds with the things I believe in that I could not feel at home with him. I surely do not want to be used by him or to estrange other acquaintances from me by making them think that I am thick with him. Yet I do not want to hurt his feelings unnecessarily. Neither do I want to be unfaithful to my self-motivation to be kind and respectful. Shall I drive him home? How shall I talk to him if I do so? Should I make him feel that this ride can only be an exception? In this case there is no quick and spontaneous response. Original discretion has to operate rather consciously. I must weigh all aspects of the matter deliberately.

Our analysis of original discretion thus far may give the mistaken impression that we must involve ourselves in lengthy and agonizing appraisals before every original decision we make. This is not the case. Often the elements of original discretion play their role so quickly that they remain unnoticed. They seem spontaneous and intuitive. It is indeed one of the demands of original discretion that a situation be given no more attention than it is worth. If we do otherwise, we tax our original resources unwisely. We go against our original limitations. We become so anxious and vigilant that we cannot be our original selves. Fortunately for us, in many cases the whole process of original discretion takes place on a preconscious level.

Why can original discretion operate so swiftly? Because by many previous appraisals of the same nature, made in similar situations, I have formed distinct self-motivations that reflect concrete modes of faithfulness to my originality in regard to specific situations. Many situations I face are quite in line with the ones I have faced before. I do not start all over again each time I face, for example, the possibility of betraying my original calling when some wild-eyed orator or social agitator defiantly shouts at me from a rostrum what is best for me. I spontaneously exercise free choice in regard to the kind of social contribution I can make best to society, one to which I have been self-motivated for a long time. I can say, therefore, that I "am" my self-motivations. My self-motivations are the momentum I have freely built into my life.

I should also realize that original discretion is not always concerned with tasks that are arduous, harmful, or heroic. It is also concerned with fun, pleasure, and enjoyment. Loyalty to the true me implies also that I indulge in the typical pleasures that relax and recreate the unique kind of person I happen to be. Often the best response to what I truly am may be to take a nap, a swim, have a drink, read a mystery story, enjoy the comics, go to the movies, or bask in the sun. All of my life—labor and leisure, pain and pleasure, solitary reflection and human encounter—must continue to unfold my originality and self-motivation.

At some periods of history, conventional wisdom may deteriorate into pedantics; it becomes so detailed that it seems to predict beforehand every detail of life. There seems to be no room left for personal orientation in tune with one's originality. Being overpowered in the name of conventional wisdom was perhaps a danger in the recent past, but not so much today. Nowadays, original discretion can be paralyzed in a far more subtle fashion. In the past I found myself alone to scan the practical sides of my concrete life situation. Today countless experts are crowding in on me, each one with his own advice. Professionals, how-to-do-it books, organizations, and public media bombard me with minute admonitions about every detail of life. I must be wise enough to take their suggestions into account without allowing them to take over the function of original discretion. Original discretion takes their words as seeds for insights, nothing less and nothing more.

We must rid our mind of the idea that any expert knows ultimately better than we ourselves how to live our lives. Surely, he may tell us how the average man lives his life and what endangers his happiness. We should heed such information. What the expert cannot tell us is how to make this information operational in the unique situation of our personal lives. There we alone are the experts. We alone are responsible. If we go wrong there, we can never reproach the expert. It was our decision, not his, to abandon our responsibility—to leave it all up to the pundits or the public.

We must learn to shut the experts and the public out when we are on the verge of making the personal decisions that will motivate and shape our future. It is absurd to want a personal life as successful as others or one which would meet public approval or receive the blessing of psychiatrists, sociologists, psychologists, column writers, or TV commentators. If their word has become our criterion, we no longer lead a life that can be called ours. The pronouncements of the pundits would be the main motivation of our actions and decisions; it would be their life not ours. We would have lost our power of original discretion. True liberation occurs when public information is dissolved into the fully personal and when public ideologies about how to live our lives are discarded as the pedantic pretentions they are.

Self-Motivation and Compulsive Drive

When I do try to live in original discretion, I may become aware of an opposite tendency in me, one which interferes with the flexibility of self-motivation. Human originality seeks its way in this world sensitively and playfully. But I may also experience in myself a tyrannical drive toward obsessive thoughts and feelings, stereotyped judgments, toward words and deeds that do not take into account the uniqueness of persons and situations. This drive makes me insensible and inflexible. I repeat certain reactions no matter how ill adapted. Such insensitive reactions block the easy and spontaneous flow of my self-motivated life. They play havoc with my relations with others. They make me say things I will regret. My judgment becomes extreme, out of touch with the limited problem with which I am dealing.

Under the influence of these emotional laden reactions, I make decisions harmful for my growth and happiness. Such drives emerge somewhere deep inside me. As an infant I had to orient myself toward the people and things around me. I was not yet able to reflect quietly on myself and my relations with others. At times I felt overwhelmed by envy, greed, possessiveness, panic, rage. These sentiments compelled me to react in a fixed way. For example, I tried to defy the power of my father or mother by blind rebellion. Or I wanted to placate them by blind submissiveness. Or I stubbornly did my own thing no matter how they felt. I still may do that today. Instead of being flexible, I cling fanatically to one opinion, expression, or pattern of behavior. In and through it, I pit my whole self against the others. I hang on to it for dear life. Nobody can reach me at that moment. The real me is frozen in this one expression. It has to be thawed out before my original self can begin to be touched by the more delicate nuances of reality.

These powerful feelings of childhood, and the reactions they gave rise to, have become unconscious. The only sign of their appearance is the self-defeating behavior that suddenly bursts forth in certain situations. Inexplicably I find myself spouting angry denunciations or tightening up in the midst of a conversation. My words become absolute; I keep stubbornly insisting on a point, driving it home relentlessly. I find myself unable to remain sensitive to the feelings of others. A kind of obsession keeps me captive of this urge to violent repetition of the same excessive opinion.

Sometimes I may confuse true originality with this manifestation of quasi originality. The reason for this confusion is not far to seek. I feel that these one-sided reactions emerge somewhere in my personality. I may be tempted to say: "That's the typical me; it's too bad, but people should take me as I am." But is it the real me? Or is it a tenacious remnant of an infantile response to the behavior of adults that could not be understood or digested by me as a child? Doing my own thing is frequently confused with doing my infantile thing; this is not really the truly original me. If anything, these outbursts block my motivational growth.

Enlightened loyalty to my originality implies the discovery and resolution of these compulsive drives. Once I begin to live the ease and flexibility of human originality, I may recognize the moments when I lose my relaxed self-orientation, when these undigested sentiments of the past take over. The next step is to identify what in a situation gives rise to these feelings. The best way might be to compare the situations in which I remember that the same reaction took my freedom away. I may then find the constant element that brought on the same behavior. As soon as I detect this element, I can reflect on it. I can ask myself what are the hidden feelings behind it? I can play with all kinds of hypotheses about the chain that binds my reaction to the incident that evokes it. I may go back in my history and try to remember how and when similar things happened to me. I may not be able to reach back to the beginning of childhood where it probably all started. Fortunately, it is not necessary to know the ultimate childhood incident or relationship that is at the root of my rigidity. Sometimes preoccupation with the beginnings of compulsive conduct may blind me to my present responsibility. I may put all the blame on my childhood. I refuse to obtain self-knowledge by reflecting on my problems as they show themselves here and now.

In the light of increasing self-understanding, the hold of infantile compulsions on my life may diminish. Self-motivation may take the place of compulsive drive. In some cases, however, the hold of the past may be so strong that I must seek professional help. The power of such reactions is the strongest force I may have to cope with in my search for an original life. Its strength is due to its origin in infancy and to the fact that it eludes conscious awareness.

Cultural Orientation and Originality

Another power that inhibits my original unfolding is that of the value-orientations of my culture. Often these directions are communicated to me at a stage later than infancy. It may therefore be less difficult to make them available to my consciousness. This is not to say that I am spontaneously aware of the inhibiting force of cultural orientations. Usually I am so identified with my culture that I do not realize how its tendencies may hamper my self-unfolding. For growth in original discretion it is thus necessary to reflect on this specific cultural obstacle to living a self-motivated life.

There is a view of culture that may incline us to betray unwittingly our own originality. The person who holds this view places on a pedestal the orientation of the cultural period in which he happens to live. He takes for granted that his own time is the best possible time of all. He urges himself and everyone else to live up to its popular norms. He never asks himself if each type of person can live by what is popular in a specific period of human history.

Society today highly regards the practical, functional, and scientific spheres of life. For mankind at this moment of its evolution, this regard may be necessary. However, it does not follow that all men should participate in such concerns equally all the time. Would this not be the worst thing that could happen to a culture? Certain activities may be worth while for most people. They may be exceedingly important for this moment of the human evolution. Yet some men, because of their original predisposition, should not engage in them.

Let us look more closely at the meaning of culture. At the beginning of humanization, tribal man had discovered only a few values and facts; he could live these harmoniously without too much conflict. In the beginning of history, for example, man did not face the conflict between informational living and openness to deeper values. Harvesting, seeding, hunting, and dancing were practical means for survival. At the same time, he embodied his worship in them. Tribal man experienced these functional activities as harmoniously interwoven with the survival of his tribe, the care of his family, the worship of his gods. Practical and aesthetic values were welded similarly. He expressed his aesthetic delight in dancing, in the carvings on his tools, in the designs on the walls of his cave. Long before the functional and technical era, man's original openness to human values and their incarnation in cultural acts was facilitated by a certain inner unification of life.

Contemporary man has progressed greatly in functional, informational, technical, and scientific development. He has built an impressive body of skills and knowledge. This specialization, however, may blind him to those human values that should sustain and guide his life. The functional and informational may preoccupy him to such an extent that he forgets about the values that are at the heart of his life and civilization.

Tribal man was able to live the main values of life in such a way that his commitment to one value did not obscure other values for him. This situation changed as man moved toward urbanization. He formed the first small collective units housing members of different tribes, each one contributing the insights and information gathered by his people. The store of skills and knowledge increased enormously. Specialization became necessary. No longer could each man handle the knowledge available for each cultural activity. People were needed who would spend the major portion of their day in dedication to the unfolding of one or the other of these increasingly complex dimensions of human existence. Craftsmen became involved in practical enterprises. They often had less time to devote to aesthetic and scientific values. Artists in turn were dedicated to preservation of the aesthetic appreciation. They were less involved in the unfolding of practical values. Other modes of value-orientation evidence the same concentration in one area of value-radiation to the diminishment of others.

There was only one way for post-tribal culture to safeguard the actual or at least potential commitment of its members to all fundamental human values. It had to foster the emergence in its midst of centers of value-radiation. The culture as a whole became a field of centers of value-radiation—forces which kept each other and the cultural field as a whole in a precarious balance. People predisposed to develop a specific human value could free themselves from other involvements. They had the time and economic freedom to witness for this value in special intensity. They kept its wealth alive for other members of the same culture who needed the complementary influence of the values witnessed for in such centers of value-radiation. Thus, in a given culture we might find people set free for scientific endeavors, for the arts, and for religious presence, to mention only a few areas of concentration.

Post-tribal culture can thus be seen as a field of value forces. These centers keep each other actually or potentially in balance. The culture fluctuates in accordance with the intensity or diminution of these value centers. Culture is a dynamic field of human unfolding in time and space. The field of value forces, therefore, can be regarded both vertically and horizontally. Vertical refers to the time dimension, the history of a culture. Horizontal refers to the space dimension, the localized contemporary manifestations of a culture at a certain moment of its history. The vitality of the culture as a whole, its balance and fullness, is not necessarily present at any one moment of its history. A culture at any one moment of its history can be called full and balanced when all centers of value-radiation that represent the different fundamental values of human life are still somehow present in that culture. We do not call it actually balanced. For usually one or the other center of value-radiation is not appreciated at that moment by the population at large. Therefore, the culture as a whole is not actually balanced at any specific moment. However, the subdued but real continuation of such value centers keep the possibility alive for the neglected value to reassert itself in later periods.

Usually, the changing historical situation of a culture leads to an alternation of cultural periods. Each one of these periods is characterized by a prevalence of involvement in one or the other specific set of values. The actual radiation power of centers that sustain these popular values is great in such a period. Value centers representative of values less popular— in view of the felt contemporary and evolutional needs of the population—exert less influence at that time. Their actual radiation power is dimmed.

We could thus describe culture as a dynamic, potentially balanced unfolding of a population over a long span of time. A paradox presents itself. Not the popular but the unpopular centers of value-radiation are crucial for the maintenance and unfolding of the culture. The reason is not hard to find. When we look on culture as a dynamic whole unfolding in history, we do not feel concerned about the values that are highly popular in a specific period of its development. These take care of themselves, as it were. They are lived and articulated enthusiastically in a given cultural period. However, a cultural period tends by its nature to be one-sided.

Our long-range concern should be for the forgotten values, values that are unpopular, neglected, perhaps ridiculed and rejected. People possessed by the violence of envy may try to destroy not only the actuality but even the future potentiality of the values that are momentarily rejected by their culture. They may silence the lonely prophet of forgotten values among them. The temporarily underestimated value should be kept alive in some witnesses if these values are to be renewed in later generations. Sooner or later a change will take place in the historical situation. The once-hidden value may recapture its meaning and importance in the desire and imagination of the population.

Thus the balanced unfolding of the culture as a historical whole calls for the continuation of centers of value-radiation that at present are not popular. The survival of the temporarily neglected human value is of vital importance. There may be a time in history, such as our own, when many chance factors and the logic of human evolution foster development of functional knowledge. In such a time people and institutions are liable to be carried away by the scientific, technical, and practical values of human unfolding. The centers that radiate these values become more popular than ever. Many co-operate in this advancement of technical knowledge. Partly because of genuine interest in these values. Partly because co-operation assures increase in status, power, and possession. Centers that radiate other values, like the aesthetic and the philosophical, may lose popular support. Their supporters dwindle. Their few adherents do not receive a tangible remuneration. The light such centers may have shed in times past is dimmed by other stars appearing now brightly in the firmament of the culture.

A civilization could be carried away by the one-sidedness characteristic of a cultural period. It may structure its whole scale of values around the values that temporarily fascinate the imagination. What about those citizens who cannot experience presently central values as central in their own personality? Whose originality does not imply a spontaneous affinity for these values? They may pretend to themselves and others that the popular values are central also in their lives. But they cannot experience these values as central in a truly original way. They deceive themselves. Such deception becomes a force of self-alienation in their personality. It is the fate of their uniqueness to live and radiate a value orientation momentarily neglected by the culture. They cannot find true self-motivation in the popular direction, for it is not theirs.

Each man should be encouraged to be his original self. In this way we guarantee the presence also of people who stand for the forgotten values of humanity in a specific cultural period. In fact, those people may be more deeply and sincerely dedicated to these forgotten values than some of those who lived and worked for them in former periods when they were popular.

The one-sidedness of a cultural period is a threat and a promise of purification in regard to the values a culture plays down temporarily. Cultural one-sidedness threatens the survival of certain essential values. The same one-sidedness may purify the temporarily dismissed radiation center of the threatened value. It no longer attracts those who came mainly for the status, power, or possession that went with its popularity. In times when these values were popular, the latter incentives may have outweighed the incentive of personal commitment to this value as value because of genuine self-motivation.

I can thus look at my own cultural period in two ways. I can exalt it in my imagination as the perfectly balanced period. I can also live in the conviction that my own cultural period is necessarily one-sided and defective as all other periods have been. I am aware that my own norms of success are as narrow-minded, provincial, and prejudiced as those of the cultural period in which I happen to live. Therefore, I can bear with the originality of my wife, children, friends, students, or colleagues—even if this implies for them, and perhaps indirectly for me, less economic gain, status, and popularity at the present time.

A teacher of psychology may belittle the original interest of a student engaged in a more humanistic study of man. The cultural period in which he happens to live likes better the kind of psychology that follows the methods of the physical sciences. This is not to say that the teacher should tell the student to forget about the kind of psychology that temporarily fascinates people. That would be unrealistic.

Students will have to work with people and within situations that have patterned themselves after the contemporary scale of values and meanings. Moreover, a one-sidedly fostered value is still a value. As such, it is one possible contribution to the culture and worthy to be known. This is only to say that the teacher should—over and above this—respect the other genuine interests of his students, even if they do not tie in with trends that are popular.

Always keep in mind the essential provincialism of any culture or counterculture. Then you dare to foster unfamiliar trends without shame or guilt. Not all people should be equally involved in the concerns and values of a passing period of their culture. A genuine interest that is at odds with those of society today should not be killed off. "Odd" interests may keep alive cultural values that are neglected. Be faithful to a value that means much to you, if only little to your colleagues in the office or your cronies on the golf course. You may be called by your own originality to keep this neglected or forgotten interest alive, even if this may not make you rich or popular in the incidental phase of the culture or counterculture in which you happen to be born.